PUBLICITY
HOW TO GET IT

*the text of this book is printed
on 100% recycled paper*

PUBLICITY
HOW TO GET IT

Richard O'Brien

BARNES & NOBLE BOOKS

A DIVISION OF HARPER & ROW, PUBLISHERS

New York, Hagerstown, San Francisco, London

A hardcover edition of this book is published by Harper & Row, Publishers, Inc.

First BARNES & NOBLE BOOKS edition published 1978

ISBN: 0-06-463465-5

79 80 81 82 10 9 8 7 6 5 4 3 2

Contents

Introduction

Publicity: How to Get It is precisely that: a "how to" book spelling out all the possible ways to obtain publicity, and how to do it without hiring a professional publicist.

It has long been my conviction, in over fifteen years as a press agent, that many of my clients, even though amateurs in the field of publicity, could have done the job better, if they'd had the time and the inclination (as well as the rhinoceros hide necessary to withstand personal rejection). No one could know more about himself than a client; certainly no one could be more interested in himself than a client; if his mind is restless enough, no one can think up more avenues of self-promotion than a client.

Furthermore, in the past ten years it has become incontestably evident that publicity can be obtained by anyone. Remember all those suddenly sprung activist organizations that received so much instant media coverage in the 1960s? Newspapers, magazines, radio, and television are hungry for new ideas.

Publicity is the means of spreading new ideas, and today anyone, no matter how obscure initially, can disseminate information if (a) he knows how to do it and (b) the information he wants to make known has news value.

So I have no trepidation in telling you, the amateur, the perhaps as yet untried publicist, that you can do the same job that people have been paying me to do for years. Once you're past learning the few basic tricks, all it takes to keep you going is drive or, if you lack drive, your own good conscience and willpower.

This book explains those few basic tricks, from how one determines the news value of the product, event, or person he is trying to publicize, to how to go about getting that news out. In an effort to keep the reader (and author) awake, I have at times used what I perhaps indulgently think of as humor in my examples of press releases, biographies, etc. However, even when the effort seems flippant, the actual "how to" structure of that effort is dead serious and just as enlightening as if I'd written it with straight face and stifled yawn.

If this book has one underlying theme, it is the underlying theme of every good press agent. To publicize well, you must touch all the bases; you must make every effort to reach every possible press outlet available to you. If as a press agent, pro or amateur, you're going to allow yourself to be lazy, then you might as well start now—stop reading and settle down for a nice, cozy nap.

However, if you want to promote yourself, or a friend, or have been designated to serve as press agent for a group or an individual, if you want to find out what publicity is all about and whether it might be the career you've been looking for, if you're a professional publicist who wonders if he's covering all his bets, then this book is for you. Good luck with it. The ideas contained within have certainly been good luck for me.

Richard O'Brien

February, 1977

PUBLICITY

HOW TO GET IT

1

Publicity: What It Is and How to Get It

Like most people, I have often been asked—at social gatherings, during bus-stop acquaintanceships, and when all else has flagged: "What kind of work do you do?"

For over fifteen years I have been answering, "Publicity," and that's usually when the going begins to get muddy.

"That sounds like a very interesting job," they say. "How long have you been in advertising?"

No, no, I hasten to assure them. I am *not* in advertising. I am in publicity. There is a world of difference.

"Oh, really? What *is* the difference?"

And I begin to explain, but most of the time, as I watch eyes slowly glaze, I know I'm not getting my message across. I just hope I can do it better here, with you.

There is one major difference between publicity and advertising. In advertising, the client pays both the advertising agency and the medium in which the advertisement is to be placed. In publicity, the client pays only the publicist.

To clarify this: In advertising, a client pays an advertising agency to work up and place an ad. He also pays for the ad. In publicity, a client pays a publicity agency to create publicity. He does not pay for the resultant publicity, whether it appears in newspapers, magazines, radio, television, or what have you. That part comes free.

The reason for this is simple. Publicity is the art of furnishing or even creating news. People don't charge you when you give them news. They're eager for it, and quite willing, at their own expense, to disseminate it.

Publicity also has one major advantage over advertising. People, when reached by advertising, often have a skeptical attitude toward it. After all, someone is trying to sell them something. What is his angle?

Publicity, on the other hand, reaches them in the form in which they receive all other news. There is no indication that anyone is advertising anything. It bears the imprimatur of the medium it appears in, and thus appears to be, and usually is, solid, straight information that can be regarded as unvarnished truth.

Publicity is a field that is very much of our time. We live in a world of communication, and publicity is exactly that: a communication of a fact or set of facts. Not too many years ago, publicists were viewed with great suspicion by the press. There is still some of this around (and occasionally with good reason), but, more and more, publicists are viewed as useful adjuncts to the press. They function in a manner similar to the old "leg men": people who come up with a basic news story which is then refined by the professionals.

Without publicity men and women, the world would be unaware of myriad activities that are found daily in the press or on the air.

News of political activities, of inventions, of new businesses, of local community activities, of gossip about movie stars, in-depth interviews with scientists, athletes, authors . . . take away the publicist, the press agent, and much of this would suddenly disappear.

Because the press agent is just that: an agent of the press. He fills a need, and the wise editor uses him well.

There are some basic principles employed in gaining publicity. These are principles to be used by anyone seeking publicity, whether the veteran professional or the knees-a-quivering tyro.

The first is to become thoroughly familiar with whatever it is you wish to publicize. The more you know about something, the more potential news there is in it.

The second is to decide where to publicize this news.

The third is to do it.

Simple enough, and with good reason. Publicity is really a very simple job. All it requires is a little intelligence, a little insight, a fair amount of tact, and a great deal of push.

Don't misunderstand me on the latter. I don't mean that one has to be terribly aggressive, in a pushy sense, when dealing with the press. Some of the best press agents are strictly soft-sell. What I mean by "push" is simply that quality of not giving up, of going after everything there is to go after, as quickly and efficiently as you can.

Those are the basics. Now how does publicity actually work?

Principally in two ways: via the typewriter and the telephone.

There are essentially three things the publicist uses his type-writer for: press releases (also known as news releases), letters, and photo captions. A show business publicist, such as myself, will also use it constantly for column items.

A press release is basically a news story. It even has a headline, just like the stories you see in your local newspaper.

A letter is used by the press agent to inform an editor, a re-porter, or a booker for a radio or TV show. It's usually used when the press agent is hoping for a story on the client he represents. It succinctly presents the news angle or angles on the client.

Photo captions are just that: captions used beneath the photos that the publicist sends out to the press.

Column items are the smallish paragraphs that appear in the news space taken up by a columnist. Sometimes the columnist writes the entire column himself. Often, though, he relies on press agents for much of his material.

The phone, of course, is more versatile than the typewriter. It can function as a press release when the press agent simply calls in his story. More often, it is used the way a letter is used: to apprise the person on the other end about the publicist's client— ideally to so entice that other person that there is an on-the-spot agreement to use the client or materials about the client. Most of the time, however, a follow-up letter or news release has to be sent. Then the phone is used again to follow up the follow-up. If persistence is the name of the game in publicity (and it is!), then the phone is an even more useful tool for the publicist than the typewriter, since it is with the telephone that he can be (but always discreetly) the most persistent. It is wise to remember, when doing publicity, that people are basically lazy. They don't want to do any more than they have to. It's much easier to say no to a press agent, to not call him back, to drop his release in the wastebasket or file it under a batch of papers. Therefore, it's the job of the press agent to nudge, and cajole, and remind. Sometimes the man at the other end of the line says yes. Sometimes he says no. But without a call to ask him, to remind him, he would, in too many cases, have said—and done—nothing.

One of the best things about the business of publicity is its simplicity. It is so simple that the most complex machine in the world could never do it. It is a very human job. An absolute requirement of publicity is that one person deal with another person. That is the only way it can be done.

Furthermore, no specialized training is needed to become a publicist. None of the people I've known in my area of the business ever took a course in public relations in college. Some of them never even finished college. In fact, it's not really stretching it to say that once you've learned to read and write, you're eligible. (This is as true for women as it is for men. Publicity is a field that appears to have no sex barriers.)

Because it's so personal, publicity is a job that can often be done at home. Some of the top press agents work out of their apartments. Most clients don't care what you work out of, so long as you get the job done, and all it requires is a typewriter, a telephone, some basic office supplies. So if working at home is your cup of tea, then why not? But if you prefer an office—well, certainly you may rent a grandiose suite of rooms and decorate them to the utmost refinements of your taste, but all you really need is a good-sized broom closet. In my early years in publicity, I was handling some of the top names in the entertainment world in a thirteen-by-nine-foot office that housed myself, two employees, and three good-sized desks.

There are many rewards in publicity. Some, obviously, are financial, but the amateur publicist can share in all the rest of them. Not many jobs bring such quick and evident and satisfying results. To publicize a play, for example, and see the newspapers and magazines full of stories about it, to see the photos you've sent out appear in print, to book the play's stars, author, director, or producer on one radio and television show after another, and to see the effect in a jump at the box office—to have all this happen, and know that it is through your work that it happened, is very satisfying indeed. Particularly when everyone involved with the enterprise begins to lavish you with praise. And believe me, in the flush of success, people are not stinting with their praise. Of course, there are the bad times, and the grumblings . . . but this isn't the place to go into that.

One last point: If you do a good job, you're going to wind up with a number of press clippings—news stories, column items, pictures, feature interviews, listings of TV and radio appearances. What to do with them?

If you're publicizing yourself, there's no problem. You either keep them or you don't. But if you're doing publicity for someone else—the local PTA, a politician, a charity auction, a theater group—then it's a good idea to let people know just what kind of a job you've done for them. It may also be a good idea to hang on to at least some of those clippings, as you may be able to use them as a lever for further publicity. Some press agents keep a scrapbook for each client, and every so often show him his clippings. I prefer to send my clients an envelope every week with all their clippings, buying second copies or making reproductions of important stories for my own files. The point is, you should keep the clippings at least until the people who would be interested in the work you've done have seen them. So don't just assume that because you've seen a release in the local paper, everyone else has too. Save it and show it to them.

2

What Publicity Can Do for You

I think just about everyone is aware that publicity can be helpful, but perhaps not as many realize just how helpful it can be.

Publicity can help turn an unknown into a millionaire; a book overlooked or disparaged by reviewers into a runaway best-seller; a game which could easily have been ignored into the nation's hottest; a singer who might have appealed only to the ladies into an entertainer who captures both sexes triumphantly.

Conversely, adverse publicity has helped spell the end for many a career and product.

The key word is "help." Woody Allen couldn't have become a world-famous comedian if he hadn't been brilliantly funny, but the publicity value of the newspaper, magazine, radio and TV interviews, the continual barrage of column items, and the advertising tie-ins all helped to move his career along at a much faster pace than it would have without this help, and it's even a moot point as to just how far even so brilliant a funnyman would have been able to go without the help of that early publicity.

Jacqueline Susann is an outstanding case of someone who believed in publicity and made it work for her. Her devotion to publicizing her books was legendary in the business. She did all the radio and TV shows, all the print (newspapers, magazines, etc.), all the personal appearances in bookstores, crossing the country over and over again to "sell" her books. She would walk into bookstores and get to know the sales help so they'd be more willing to sell her books. She even rearranged the displays of her books to make them more prominent. Did it work? One would have to assume so. The books were not acclaimed by most critics as literary gems, and though word of mouth might possibly have made them successful anyway (the best of publicity can't sell something that people just plain don't want or like), it's highly unlikely that word of mouth alone would have done the trick. In any event, it's absolutely certain that Jacqueline Susann didn't think so.

A friend of mine, Bill Kaufman, once handled publicity for a game called Twister for the Milton Bradley Company. The game, as you may remember, consisted of a vinyl mat with a series of gaily colored circles printed on it, and a large cardboard with a spinner on it. Two to four people in stocking feet would stand on the mat and do as directed by a referee who spun the dial. The pointer would indicate upon which colored disks the players must put their arms and legs. The resultant entanglements could be fun, and Bill and the other people at the company he worked with came up with a campaign which included, among a number of other things, an appearance on the *Tonight* show and a promotion in Fort Lauderdale which would make use of vacationing college students.

Johnny Carson and Eva Gabor played the game for six minutes or so on the show, and the next day many major department stores and outlets were besieged by people who wanted "the game Johnny Carson and Eva Gabor played last night."

With the aid of the city of Fort Lauderdale, which presumably preferred having the college students play Twister than do other things they might have found to occupy themselves with, Bill got several hundred students to play the game while two Miami television stations, a UPI photographer, and staff photographers from the Miami *Herald* and the Fort Lauderdale *News* recorded the results. The UPI photos broke nationally, the Miami *Herald* ran a two-page photo story, the Fort Lauderdale *News* carried a photo feature, the TV shows ran their film. Finally, there was the actual word of mouth from the students who played the game and went back home to tell their friends about it.

With these as the two salient thrusts of the campaign, along with a great deal of additional publicity, by late summer Twister became, according to *Toy and Hobby World,* the nation's number-one-selling game.

Bing Crosby, who may still be the biggest total record-seller of them all, was a crooner when he came up, and it was feared that as a romantic balladeer he might turn off too much of the male audience, who would think of him as a sissy. Bing's press agent, the story goes, thought of a simple expedient. Have Bing become known as a habitué of the racetrack, an improver of the breed. Pictures were taken of Bing at racetracks, jokes were inserted in his radio programs about the dubious quality of his horses, and, presumably as a result of all this, his status as a certified macho was graven in stone. Certainly, few performers have ever had Crosby's universal appeal, and I personally never came across any of the questioning regarding the Old Groaner that I did about many other popular singers of the day.

On the other hand, if it hadn't been for bad publicity, silent screen comedian Fatty Arbuckle would almost certainly have remained a star, the Edsel might have been able to stick around long enough to get the bugs out, and George Romney, George McGovern, and Edmund Muskie might have been far more successful in their bids for the Presidency.

Publicity is certainly not necessarily the be-all and the end-all, but it can be of immeasurable help when used properly. Furthermore, if you do it yourself, it is the cheapest form of "advertising" in the world. It costs you no more than paper, stamps, envelopes, phone calls, and your time.

Let me also mention that there are two basic forms of publicity: for-the-moment, and institutional. An example of the first would be publicizing an engagement at a nightclub.

Back in the 1960s, among the many nightclubs I handled was

one in Greenwich Village known as the Bitter End. Acts there were changed frequently: every week or two, usually. We would send out releases, column items, and pictures of the entertainers, get reviewers down, set up interviews for the performers concerned. That publicity was for-the-moment.

However, we often arranged for major stories on the club itself. As a breeding place for bright new talent, it justified the ensuing articles on the club and its owner. Since these articles usually were written several weeks or months in advance of their publication, there was no way of getting in just who would be appearing at the club the week or month the article came out. So this publicity was institutional. It let people know that such a club existed, that it was, in its way, a major institution, and that they could rely on it for good entertainment at reasonable prices. Thus, a visitor to New York, or even a New Yorker himself, might choose to trek down to the Village not to see a specific performer, but to visit the club itself. For anything that's going to be around for a while, institutional publicity is just as important as the day-to-day variety.

One final note. A publicist is in many ways a salesman. As with any salesman, he is at his most effective when he believes in what he is selling. If you are asked to publicize something you don't believe in, my advice is either don't publicize it, or investigate it till you find an aspect of it that you do believe in and then sell your story from that angle. You'll be much more successful, and you'll certainly feel much better about yourself.

3

Planning a Campaign

If you asked me, my initial reaction would be that planning a campaign is a seat-of-the-pants thing. I have an idea of what I want, I know what I need to get, and I go after it, cramming in as much as I can the first day, cramming in as much as I can the second day, cramming in as much as I can the third day, etc.

But of course I do it with an instinct trained by fifteen years of experience. Without that experience, you may need a little more time to gather your wits. So here's an indication of how to go about planning your campaign.

Know what it is you're publicizing. Have your news angle or angles in mind.

Think of the places which might be interested in your news. Make a list of them. Remember that if your client is considered ineligible by one department in a newspaper, he may be right for another department. So also make provisional subheadings. Go through files, books, or anything else you may have that will mention other possible outlets. Add them to your list. If you know others who can give you advice in this direction, get it from them.

Decide which are the most important. Go after them first.

Sometimes the most important things are the big things. Sometimes, because you realize it would be best to build your campaign from the ground up, the most important things are the small things—an interview with the local weekly paper, a trade-journal story, a minor local radio show. The first two give you hard news stories that you can add to your publicity kit, stories that might interest an editor at a bigger publication who wouldn't give you a nod without them. The third gives your client a radio credit and, sometimes even more importantly, gives him some on-the-air experience so that by the time he's ready in a news sense for a bigger radio or TV shot, he'll also be ready as an interviewee.

Some interview shows, in fact, insist on what's known as a pre-interview. A pre-interview is the name for a procedure wherein a member of a show's staff does an off-the-air interview with your client (or you, if you're your own client) in order to see if he has what it takes to interest an audience. The advice here is that the client should come well armed with his facts and have as many anecdotes as possible to tell in connection with his story. Interview shows generally look for human interest, and anecdotes are an important form of human interest.

If you like, you can go after all the TV first, or all the radio, or all the newspapers, etc. I prefer to scatter my shots—some press interviews, some magazines, some radio and TV. Since people at newspapers seem to differ from people at magazines, just as both differ from their counterparts in radio and TV (who have their own separate personalities), the variety keeps things a little more interesting, and it also keeps your client from saying, when you tell him you have interviews set with the *New York Times,* the *National Observer,* the *Washington Post, Time,* and *Newsweek,* "What about radio and TV?"

However, one of the best things about publicity is that there are no hard and fast rules, except the ones of persistence and an obsessive eye to detail. If you're sure the best way to kick off your client's publicity is with a barrage of stunts, then go to it. If column items seem the absolute best course to pursue in the opening weeks, give them a whirl—you could be right. The only major thing to remember is to find out what all the possibilities are and go after them, all of them, as quickly as you can. And when and if you've gone after them all, your next step is to define what all the new possibilities are. Because new possibilities always exist. New radio shows, new magazines, new departments in a newspaper, or new editors to replace the ones who turned you down, new angles on your client that could mean approaching a whole new area you never could approach before. Those new angles sometimes open up because something has changed with your client, or because he's given you information you didn't have before. New angles can also spring up because you hadn't thought of them before. In fact, as long as you keep thinking, new angles will always spring up.

"A campaign" really means deciding what to go after and going after it. If you do both, and do them well, the odds are you'll be delighted with the results.

4

How to Determine Your Outlets

If you're planning to go somewhere, it's obviously a good idea to know ahead of time where you're going. So it is with publicity. To work effectively—which is to say, by touching every base possible —you have to know what your publicity outlets are: all the areas that may be receptive to what you're trying to publicize.

There is a variety of places to turn. One of the most obvious, of course, is your local newspaper. However, in a city of any size, there is usually more than one newspaper. There may be one, two, or more daily newspapers and then, quite possibly, a number of weekly newspapers that cover specific portions of the general area the daily newspapers reach.

In New York City, for instance, there are, at this writing, three daily newspapers and some forty to forty-five weekly newspapers. Some of the weeklies, like the *Village Voice* and the *SoHo News,* are city-wide in scope. Others, like *Flatbush Life* and the *Rockaway Record,* are strictly local in coverage. A few are foreign-language publications.

Television and radio are also obvious publicity outlets. News shows, interview shows, and public-service bulletins provide ready potential for the publicist.

Next are magazines, some local, many national. Included in

magazines would be newspaper Sunday supplements—some, such as *Parade* and *Family Weekly,* distributed nationally, with huge circulations. Then there are trade journals—magazines and newspapers devoted to a single subject, like the *Hollywood Reporter* and *Variety* for the entertainment industry, *Adhesives Age,* which, one would assume, covers the universe of stick-to-it-iveness, and *Dog World,* the cat's meow of its field. Trade journals, in all their varieties, forms, and esoterica, number close to 20,000 in this country alone.

There are also newspaper syndicates and wire services, which send their stories to newspapers across the country and sometimes throughout the world. The Associated Press's news, for instance, goes to 1,260 subscribing newspapers in the United States and, in addition, to a number of foreign nations.

But knowing all this in just a general way is not particularly helpful. For instance, if you have a story on a local PTA fund-raising affair—a bake sale, to be more specific—to whom do you send this story at your daily newspaper? Let's see if I can break it down for you.

If your story is about a PTA fund-raising project, then, unless your paper has an education page, it is strictly a news story. It does not fall, for example, under the category of amusements, sports, editorial, business, books, bridge, cameras, stamps, classifieds, travel, or, one hopes, obituaries.

So off it shall go to the news department. But to whom in the news department does one send it? To the Editor, to the City Desk, to the Local News Desk (as opposed to National News Desk), to a specific name?

If there is a Local News department in your daily newspaper, this is where it should go. In the case of something like a PTA release, it would be best to call the paper and ask for the Local News editor, tell him about what you're planning to send, and ask if he's the right person. Sometimes he's not. He may have an assistant who handles that aspect of his department. Or he may be about to go off on vacation (you'd be amazed at the odd times people take off for vacations) and will suggest the name of his substitute. This way, you have a name, and if the release doesn't appear when you expect it to, you can call and ask him about it. Sometimes the mail gets lost, sometimes it gets misplaced, and more often than not your release hasn't been used because there wasn't enough space for it. In the latter case, the release is often discarded. By calling, you can sometimes save a lost story, because your personal interest is enough to make the editor take his own personal interest and see what he can do about using it in the next issue.

However, if there is no Local News department, the City Desk, if the paper is large enough, or the Editor, if it's not, would be the logical choice. Once more, the assiduous publicist would call first and find out to whom the release should be addressed. Frankly, some editors and reporters find themselves too busy for such nonsense and are sure to give you short shrift. Admittedly, that's no fun. But for the most part you'll find your question answered, and often the fact that you called in advance will make the release a little more important to its recipient when it arrives.

Now what about weekly newspapers? Your PTA story is certain to be right for a paper that covers your area exclusively. And the procedures outlined above apply. But this doesn't mean that you should confine yourself to that local paper. Often, neighboring communities are interested in what's going on near them. A paragraph about a not-that-far-away PTA sale might entice some customers from a nearby area. So check out those neighboring newspapers and see what you can do with them.

Another aid in publicizing would be a captioned picture of the bake-sale committee. Again, you would call the paper and find out where the picture should be sent. Start by asking for the Picture Desk. If that's not right, you'll soon be routed to the correct person.

It's possible there's even a feature story here. If some of the people who are donating goodies to the sale are noted for their baking, are contributing unusual items, or have some other news angle that might make them worth interviewing, you can give this area a try.

In the case of a feature story, the best person to ask for is the Feature Editor, and he, or his designate, is the person you'll try to sell your story to—by phone, by letter, or by release, and most probably by all three.

Next on your agenda would be television and radio. The trick here is to check and see what sort of programming is done by your local stations. Some radio and TV news shows feature news that is of interest to the community, even so mundane an event as a PTA bake sale. They may also have interview shows that could give your sale additional publicity. A cooking show, for instance, on which one or more of the participating mothers could give (and demonstrate) the recipes for the cakes they'll be providing at the sale. Or a discussion show for which one of your PTA members might be eligible, and on which he or she could throw in a reference to the sale.

Sometimes it's easy to check the programming (all you have to do is look in your newspaper or TV guide), and sometimes it's not. Radio programming, in particular, is touched upon only lightly, if at all, in many newspapers. Once again, the best thing to do is hie yourself to a phone. I've found that the best person to ask for at a radio station is the Program Director. He, or his assistant, can tell you what shows might be right for you, and how to approach them, or to whom you should send your release.

Even if you know exactly what shows are available to you, as is often the case with television, you still have to call and find out the contact person at each show—the one who actually gets the release or decides what guests to use. At this point, let me add that it is a very good idea to make up a directory of the names, addresses, and phone numbers of the outlets you've found (alphabetically arranged index cards have always seemed to me the simplest and most effective way of doing it), so that you or your successor will have a little easier going on the next project.

At the simplest level, there are places you can post notices on your bake sale: on telephone poles, in local shopwindows, on the grounds that surround the school. Finally, there is the mailing list. PTAs generally save postage by having the children take home the news, but even a PTA bake sale might make a little extra money if notices are mailed to people in the area who don't have children attending that particular school.

Okay. Time to drop the bake sale (unless there's a magazine in your area that actually lists such events—if so, just follow the procedures that you did with the newspapers). But before we move on, let me make it clear that the steps I've outlined in publicizing the bake sale should be followed in any publicity project, be it politics, books, theatrical productions, inventions, store openings or sales, etc.

A politician or a theater company would also go after the local paper for stories, would cultivate any weekly papers that fell into their purlieu, pursue radio and TV shows and any local magazines, send out pictures, post bills. It's just that the scope of some of these other projects would justify expanding into areas that the bake sale might not touch.

Suppose, for instance, that you have an invention and you've already gone after newspapers, magazines, radio and television in your area. Now it's time to go national.

This can be bewildering, because there are so many national outlets, and the competition is considerably keener for space in, say, *Time* magazine than in the Montclair *Times*. But if you've got a story that deserves national attention, then you can get that story told, if you try hard enough. If you are in a central area (New York City, as a prime example), many sources are immediately accessible to you. If not—well, it may make things a little tougher, but not very much, really. Remember, your main tools are the typewriter and the telephone. Your only problem is the expense of long-distance calls, and if you use your typewriter well enough, you may be receiving the long-distance calls rather than making them.

If your invention has any worth, then in all likelihood you didn't come up empty when you tried your local outlets. Releases may have broken, a feature news story may have been done, perhaps you were interviewed on radio or TV and your name and a description of your invention appeared in the listings. You have the makings of what is sometimes known as a Press (or Publicity) Kit.

A Press Kit is simply an assemblage of material that, once put together, tells the story of the product or person you are trying to publicize. Usually, when it's sent by mail, it goes out with a covering letter or note, attached to as much written and visual material as seems necessary. There should be a letter explaining succinctly about the invention and the inventor. Then a news release on the invention, and either within the same release or separately, a biography of the inventor, relating only what is pertinent to the story. Perhaps, if you have it, a photograph and/or diagram of the invention. Most important of all, if you're trying to attract national coverage, are copies of any news stories that have been done on you and your brainchild.

Now how to determine where to send all this material? Let us say that your invention is designed to dramatically reduce gasoline consumption in an automobile. There are a number of places to go with this story. First, because the automobile is used by virtually everyone, such an invention has general news interest. Because it could have, if successful, enormous business repercussions, it is also a business news story. As a new product, it can find its way to consumer departments of newspapers and magazines devoted to new products. Some of these departments use only stories about products advertised within their publication's pages, some use both advertisers and non-advertisers, and some are open to whatever strikes the editor as newsworthy. Try them all, unless you specifically know that non-advertisers are verboten. If you do have to pay for space, you'll be informed quickly enough.

Your invention would also be of great interest to general science magazines, such as *Popular Science, Mechanix Illustrated,* and *Science and Mechanics*. Next, there are a host of automotive magazines to which you could turn. How to find them? Most libraries carry reference books on publications. In this case, something like the *Standard Periodical Directory* would give you a list of several hundred journals devoted to the automobile. And from there you might move to looking up magazines devoted to science, and to business, and . . . ? The list would be almost endless, as it is for many things that are publicizable.

Again, what I've outlined as the way to pursue national publicity for an invention is also the road you must travel whenever you're seeking any kind of national publicity. Check out your local newsstands, consult reference books on periodicals and radio and television stations. Often, wire services and radio and TV networks are serviced by people in your locality. In the case of radio and TV news, if your story is good enough, a station that has a tie to a network will automatically send the story out, but it's not a bad idea to remind them by asking about it. To see if the Associated Press or United Press has "stringers" (locals who send in stories they deem nationally newsworthy) just check your local phone book. If there are none in your area, then try the nearest large city. If none there, then through a library reference book find the national headquarters and get in touch with them directly, by mail or phone. Finally, go after all the newspaper feature syndicates who might be interested in your story. An excellent source book is the syndicate edition of *Editor and Publisher*.

What is important in determining your publicity outlets is that you be diligent and enterprising. Mentally and physically seek after all possibilities; if you finally seem to have touched every last base, then, if you can, talk it over with someone. You may find he has an idea that has eluded you.

SUMMARY

1. Check your local newspapers—daily, weekly, and foreign.
2. Check local magazines, if any.
3. Get a rundown of all shows on your local radio and television stations whose programming would work the best for what you're publicizing.
4. Check out, through the library, any trade journals that might apply.

5. Do the same, via newsstands and library, on national magazines.

6. If your news is national, check out wire services and news syndicates. Sometimes you can find them listed in your local phone book. If not, try the phone book for the nearest large city, and if that fails, go after the main bureau via letter or phone, after getting their addresses and phone numbers through one of your library's reference books.

5

The News Angle: How to Find It—and Then How to Find More

In 1960 I began my life as a press agent working with a publicist named Dorothy Ross. At that time one of her accounts was a restaurant that featured Roman food, the Fontana di Trevi. It was a few days before I visited the restaurant, but in the meantime I found out all I could about it by reading the material in Dorothy's files.

Her press releases on the Fontana di Trevi were fascinating. It was obviously a restaurant of palatial appearance. A noted Italian artist had been imported to design the restaurant. The draperies, the floors, the murals, the banquettes all were rich and unique. I remember in particular a release about the bar. A well-known artisan was in the process of hand-setting thousands of individual tiles to give New York a potables counter unlike anything it had ever seen. And finally, in the rear of the restaurant was an exact replica of Rome's famous Fontana di Trevi, of *Three Coins in the Fountain* fame. Now, in New York, over three thousand miles away, people would be able to drop their coins in the Fontana's sister fountain.

The day arrived when I was to visit the restaurant. I walked in and found . . . a pleasantly decorated, intimate restaurant with a small replica of the Fontana di Trevi at the back of the room—which was perhaps thirty paces from the front of the restaurant. The bar looked like a bar. I glanced about. Everything Dorothy Ross had written about was there—but how different it seemed in reality from the glow of the written page!

Anyone who had read the press releases (and many people did, in many newspapers—they were very good releases and, as a result, a number of editors found them very newsworthy indeed) would perhaps, at first glance, have felt he'd been sold a bill of goods. Indeed, many press agents, if they'd been asked to handle the restaurant, might not have sent out more than the initial press release announcing the opening of a new restaurant. But Dorothy had imagination—not imagination in the sense of concocting something out of nothing, but in being able to look at something and see what could be done with it. A handsomely tiled bar became an artistic project worth telling everyone about; a small clay replica of a noted tourist attraction called up visions of a romance and an exotic touch that had heretofore been confined to Rome.

And Dorothy hadn't stopped there. She had found out all about the background of the owner, Armando Mei, whose family owned a restaurant that had existed for centuries in Rome. Instead of calling it simply an Italian restaurant, Dorothy made it unique in New York by disclosing that its menu would be not Italian, but Roman! Furthermore, Mei had been prominent in the underground in Italy during World War II. And the headwaiter and the bartender and the waiters all had their individual stories, many of which served as further fodder in Dorothy's quest for publicity for a pleasantly unpretentious restaurant on West 57th Street in New York City. The owner himself marveled at the publicity, and at how much she had been able to get from what was basically so little.

Dorothy's campaign worked, and the restaurant quickly became successful. Since it was an excellent restaurant, it was able to keep the business that flowed its way. It is still in operation at

151 West 57th Street, and its success inspired owner Mei to open another East Side restaurant, in this case certifiably resplendent: Iperbole, which, too, has flourished over the years.

What Dorothy had done was fully utilize one of the great tenets of publicity: Find your news angle and exploit it. And then find more. And exploit them. And then find . . .

Take, for instance, the idea of a cooperative summer day camp in the suburbs, run by the parents themselves. Your job is to publicize the camp, but why? To attract more campers? To enlist mothers in helping out? A combination of both these things, or perhaps other reasons?

Once you've decided, the first step is to determine in what way this is news, or how it can be made news. If your objective is to attract campers, the best way is to let people know that such a camp exists and, furthermore, when it is to open. This latter is necessary because an announcement of the existence of a camp has no news value; the fact that it is to open on such-and-such a date for so many weeks is news, and therefore the odds on your announcement being used by an editor are a great deal more in your favor.

Also, what are its attractions—swings, a wading pool, organized games, bus pick-up and drop-off? All can be publicized, and certainly any new equipment or features can be publicized (with future releases) as they are added, or before.

What about the people involved in the camp? What are their qualifications, their backgrounds? Is any of this newsworthy? If their backgrounds are particularly pertinent and interesting, perhaps they can even provide a feature interview in your local newspaper or on your local radio or TV station.

Additionally, whenever something new occurs within the organization—new officers, an extension of the camping season, a fund-raising activity—it too can be publicized.

What about someone who's invented something and is now prepared to market it commercially, but on a small scale? He can't afford a publicist, but feels that if he can get enough initial publicity the product will begin selling itself.

Maybe he's right. If he *is* right, it should be fairly easy to figure out just what the news angle is, and then whether perhaps there is more than one.

What is the invention? A device to save gas? Certainly timely. However, other reputed gas-saving devices have been reported and then fizzled into obscurity. Presumably they had drawbacks that kept them from really doing the job they claimed they would do. Perhaps they saved gas but destroyed the engine. Or saved gas but performed so erratically that they were ultimately a nuisance.

So, for someone with an invention that has been, in a sense, invented before, the idea would be to find out what had been wrong with all its predecessors, to spell out those defects, and then to spell out the fact that the new invention, in addition to its original news quality, is capable of doing other things as well— that is, *not* wrecking engines or being inconsistent in performance.

Also, what is the background of the inventor? What about him is interesting, particularly in the way it ties up to the invention? What spurred him on to the invention? What other devices may he currently be working on? Are there any anecdotes about things that have happened with or because of the invention? Were there other inventors in his family? What about his wife? His children? Do they have an additional story to contribute to the overall theme of the invention? In all likelihood, at least some of this will prove fodder for future publicity.

If it's a new invention, something never before invented, what is its attribute or, perhaps, attributes? What possibilities for an improvement in current life does it offer? In what way is it revolutionary? Why was it invented? Are any companies seeking to purchase it? And then, as in the above, what about the background of the inventor, what about his family, anecdotes, etc.

Let's take an actor. He's just landed a role in a play, movie, or TV show. How does he publicize this? The news angle is obviously just that: he has landed a role. For some publications, that could be enough. A hometown paper or a trade journal will often consider that news. But what is the role? What is the vehicle? Are they unusual? Do they bear some resemblance to the actor's background? Is this the first time the actor has appeared in a TV show? The third? The twentieth? This can be additional news.

Or perhaps he's a young man playing an old man, or a former director who's just turned actor, or an actor who's returned to town after appearing elsewhere for a period of time. All of these have news value and can help make a simple news release more interesting, and thus more likely to be printed.

Furthermore, his signing can be just the first release. Then there is a release about the day he's going to begin work, and finally a release on the day he's completed work. These bits of news may not always be accepted by a News Editor, but from time to time they are, and the more news angles you're armed with, the more ways you can publicize something, the better your chances for "breaking" in the media.

What about that aforementioned simple PTA bake sale? Can it be publicized? Is it worth publicizing? Certainly. It's news, and people are always looking for news. The news angle here is simply that the bake sale is going to be held on such-and-such a date, in such-and-such a location. And that may be it. But perhaps not. What is the money being raised for? For a special project? How many years has this bake sale been going on? Will any unusual cakes, pies, or cookies be on sale? Are any prize-winning bakers contributing? How many people are expected to participate? What about the officers behind the bake sale? Do they have anything unusual to contribute? What is interesting about their backgrounds?

A fledgling politician or his aides must constantly rack his brain (or their brains) for fresh angles, to keep voters interested in him straight through his campaign. A politician who peaks too soon is generally a politician who has given up on seeking fresh ideas, or new approaches to old ideas. What is his background, what are his accomplishments, what has made him become what he is? What is his approach to the issues? How does it differ from that of his opponents? What is his philosophy? How was it formed? What about his family? What are their news angles? What new issues can he talk about? What significance, if any, is there to the various places in which he appears? Who are the groups to whom he'll be speaking? Is there any relationship to be drawn between them and the candidate? And as new issues arise during the campaign, what can be made of them to the candidate's advantage?

What makes a disk jockey newsworthy? Is it his programming? His verbal approach, whether with humor, distinctive sound, machine-gun pace, or what have you? Has there ever been a music show of this kind before? What about his personality? What is distinctive about it, what separates him from the other disk jockeys in the area? What about his personal life-style, his family, friends, pets? What about his personal appearances? Is there an interesting reason why he does them? What is newsworthy about the next event? Is it an annual event? Is it for charity? Will it be for a particular organization? All of this can make a simple appearance considerably more interesting and, therefore, more likely to be picked up by the press.

By now you've probably got the idea. What initially seems to be a simple bit of news can, and usually does, have all sorts of additional dimensions.

Notice, incidentally, that publicity is usually geared to an *event*. Just as news is usually devoted to specific occurrences, so too is publicity. However, this is not always the case. Sometimes there are ongoing activities without any specific date that can also be publicized.

Perhaps you work with a clinic for people with drug problems. In addition to periodic releases announcing your existence (the news value can be simply that it is the third anniversary of the organization, or the beginning of its second six months, etc.), you can gain additional publicity by the virtue of the fact that your organization is an ongoing entity that may have interest to the community. Feature interviews in newspapers, on television and radio, in magazines and wire services are all possible.

Here the trick, again, is to find what the news angle is. In the case of a clinic for drug-users, the initial news is simply that it exists. From that we can go on to just what it does, how long it's been in existence, the results it has had—the problems, perhaps the failures, certainly the triumphs, the hopes for the future, etc. Who is best equipped to represent the clinic to the public? Usually it is the president, but in some cases there is a member of the organization who is more voluble or whose personal background is perhaps of more interest to the press. In some cases, two people—say, the "straight" president of the clinic and a former addict who now helps those in the position he formerly occupied—can be interviewed together, but in general, when going to the media, it is best to focus on a single individual.

Certainly, if an ex-addict is actively involved with the organization, his story can be of considerable interest, since specific details are always more interesting than general ones. If because of his addiction he lost his family, became a thief, wound up in jail, etc., all of this makes for a far more interesting story.

So there we are. To get publicity, you must have news. Your first job is to find that news. Your next job is to find out if there is any more news that can be added to it, to make it more interesting or perhaps to gain additional publicity.

The unusual is helpful; milestones can be publicized; anecdotes also have their place in publicity. As in everything else in life, there are many stones that can be turned over; the more you turn over, the more you increase your chances for publicity.

So get busy!

SUMMARY

1. Figure out what your news angle is by deciding on the esential quality or qualities of whatever you're hoping to promote.

2. Then find whatever subsidiary qualities can give you additional chances for promotion.

3. It sometimes helps to sit back, as if you were the editor you will be approaching, and try to judge what the newsworthiness is in the material you've assembled before you, whether physically or mentally.

6

The Press Release

The press release is one of your most important publicity tools. It *always* refers to an event, usually to a future event (though not infrequently to past events—as, say, when one of your clients wins an award without having been told in advance that he would be the recipient), and often includes a date.

The press release is usually short, rarely more than a page in length. There are several reasons for this. One is that you are trying to capture an editor's attention. A release that goes on and on is likely to lose it. The second is that only essential news is to be covered in a press release. Often that essential news requires no more than two or three paragraphs. The third is that sometimes releases are published exactly as received by a publication. It's not likely that a newspaper or magazine would want to give the space that two or more pages would take up, so if you want all the salient points of your release to be covered, you're much safer in making it all fit on one page. Otherwise, half your facts may disappear as your release is fitted to the available space.

Let's talk first about how a press release is set up, what it physically looks like.

At the top of the page, preferably at the left, should be in capital letters (so they'll be more easily seen) your name, address, and (most important of all) phone number. Never leave this heading off. This is important for two reasons. It establishes your

legitimacy (anyone who'll attach his name and address to a statement intends to stand by it) and it gives the editor or reporter a
chance to get in touch with you in case he wants to check something in your story. That is why the phone number is necessary.
Writing to you would normally take too much time or trouble. If
that's all he can do, the journalist considering your release would
be inclined to forget the whole thing. A phone call, on the other
hand, is just a matter of a few minutes, maybe even just a few
seconds. So don't forget that phone number. And if you don't have
a phone or are loath to give out your number, then just hope that
the editor has no need to check anything in your release.

Next on the page, lower down and to the right, should be an
indication of when you want the release to be published. In most
cases, you just want it published, and as soon as possible. Therefore, the best thing to write here is (in capital letters) "FOR
IMMEDIATE RELEASE, PLEASE." You can leave out the
"please" if you like, but publicity includes a bit of public relations, and it's always been my feeling that "please" can't hurt,
whereas the slightly imperious "FOR IMMEDIATE RELEASE"
might turn off a newspaperman who's having one of his grumpier
days.

Sometimes you have a specific date in mind for your release. It
could upset certain plans if the release is published too soon, so
you would then want to write something like "FOR RELEASE
APRIL 15TH, PLEASE."

But in the above case, most of the time all that you really want
to avoid is having the release printed prematurely. If you ask for
just one date, you may be asking for unnecessary trouble, since
that may be a particularly newsy day and your release will then be
bumped. Thus, you're better off putting it this way: "FOR RE-
LEASE ON OR AFTER APRIL 15TH, PLEASE."

Third in order on your page is your headline. It, too, should be
capitalized. A good headline succinctly states what the story that
follows is about. And I mean succinct. One line is the ideal, and
any more than two or three lines is asking for trouble. If an editor

finds himself bogging down in your headline, there's a good chance he'll never get to the rest of your release. Both the headline and "FOR IMMEDIATE RELEASE, PLEASE" should be underlined, since they are the two facts that must jump out at the editor: the essence of the story, and when it should be printed.

Next is the body of the release, the story you're trying to tell. The body should *always* be doubled-spaced. The reason for this is that editors and reporters often use the actual release, rather than retyping it. Thus, if there are changes or additions they wish to make in the release before it's published, they have room to do so. At this point let me also state that your release should not be crowded—there should be ample margins on both sides of the page. The reasons for this are that the release appears much more readable (and thus is more likely to be read) and that the margins can also be used for editorial corrections and instructions.

The body of the release follows exactly the rules you were taught in basic composition. There should be an opening paragraph which gives the essence of the story; a middle paragraph (or paragraphs) which tells the story in full; and a closing paragraph. (Should be, but sometimes there isn't. Sometimes there is no need for a third paragraph, or even a second, as we shall see later on.)

The five W's of journalism are helpful to keep in mind when you're writing a release. They stand for "Who," "What," "Where," "When," and "Why." The latter is not always stated, but is at least implied. For instance, a release about a singing star opening at a nightclub doesn't state why he's there. That part is understood. He's there to entertain the customers, bring in money, and keep the nightclub owner in silk shirts or, at least, twenty-five-cent cigars.

But your release should state "Who"—that is, the name of the singer; "What"—what he'll be doing, such as appearing at a nightclub singing jazz; "Where"—the name of the club and its address; "When"—the date he opens and the period of time he's going to be there.

One important thing about a press release: You want it to be as readable as possible. Therefore, it is imperative that you use a black ribbon when you type the release. Other colors are never as compelling, and they just plain don't look professional. For the same reason, use only white paper. Never date a release the way you would a letter. The date in the body of your release is good enough. That date tells the editor whether the release is still newsy. If you did send out a release two weeks or more in advance and the release was dated like a letter with the day you sent it out, an editor might glance at that date, decide your release was old news, and toss it out.

How to make copies of your release? If it's only going to one or two places, you would probably do best to just type a few originals (*never* send carbons—a carbon is less important-looking, less readable, and thus less likely to be used). If, as is more likely, you need a number of copies, there are a few alternatives. Sometimes a mimeo machine is handy to you, and sometimes a dry copier. However, I find the best-looking releases, and the least trouble, are those done by photo-offset. Photo-offset shops are ubiquitous, and their product may even be the least expensive, particularly if you count your time as an expense. At this writing, fifty copies of a release, photo-offset, cost not much more than three dollars in the New York area.

Since this book is intended for people who want to publicize many very different things, let me go on here with a number of specific examples.

Let's go back to that PTA bake sale. Let's say that it is an annual affair, and will be held on May 4 in the gymnasium of Jacksonville Elementary School. The women in charge of the affair are Wiluda Meyer, Orvaline Wynette, and Jane Smith. Only cakes, pies, and cookies baked by the mothers of the children in the school will be on sale, the proceeds will go to the school library for new books and supplies, and the sale will begin at 9:00 A.M. and end at 4:00 P.M. Here we go. (In fact, it might even be better for you to go first. Keep it all in mind, and see what you come up with. It'll be easier to remember what to do, and to keep from going wrong, if you try it first and then check yourself against my release. If this particular situation isn't what you're interested in, you could check the following ones and, when you find what you want, follow the same procedure, writing your version first, then checking it against mine. And then, unless you're just a whiz at this, rewriting it correctly. And don't forget all your headings and spacings. But I think you'll find things just naturally become clearer if you go through this chapter step by step.)

FROM: WILUDA MEYER
　　　　　123 Graceful Lane
　　　　　Jacksonville, Alabama 36265
　　　　　(205) 555-1212

FOR IMMEDIATE RELEASE, PLEASE

PTA BAKE SALE TO BE HELD MAY 4TH AT JACKSONVILLE ELEMENTARY SCHOOL

The Annual PTA Bake Sale will be held at Jacksonville Elementary School on May 4th, in the gymnasium.

The Sale will begin at 9 A.M. and continue through 4 P.M., with all proceeds being used to buy new books and supplies for the school's library. The cakes, pies, and cookies at the sale are being furnished by the parents of the school's students.

PTA members Orvaline Wynette, Jane Smith, and Wiluda Meyer, who are in charge of the event, ask that anyone interested in contributing their efforts to the sale get in touch with them through the school.

Okay, now why did I do what I did the way I did it?

The headline, for instance? Why did it leave out the gymnasium, the fact that the sale would run from 9:00 A.M. to 4:00

P.M., that the money was to be used for the library, and why did I leave out the names of the women in charge?

For one reason, and one reason only (you see, I really have nothing personal against Orvaline Wynette, whatever you might have heard). They were not necessary in the headline. The only item I left out that might be important was that the library would benefit from the sale. If the library had burned down and this was to help begin a new library, or if no library had existed before and this was to create one, then this would be important news and should be included in the headline. But in this case it's simply a routine matter of adding books and supplies, and not very newsy by itself.

However, it was very important that we mention the three things we did in the headline. If you left off the PTA bake sale, the headline would make no sense. If you substituted a less specific word—"event," for example—the headline wouldn't have enough meaning. The date, May 4, is important, because you want everyone to know when it's being held. The newspaper may cut the date out of its headline, but it's important to you (and important that the editor can immediately see when it's going to happen so he can figure out the timeliness of it), so you keep it in. Finally, it's absolutely essential that people know where the bake sale is being held, so you say "Jacksonville Elementary School." Of the five W's, four are included in this headline. "Who" is the PTA, "What" is the bake sale, "Where" is the school, and "When" is May 4. The only thing missing is "Why," which is to benefit the school library, and that's found in the body of the release.

Now what about my lead paragraph? Why did it read the way it read, and why was it written in the order it was written?

It is always best to lead off with the thing you are trying to publicize. It is what is most important to you, and should thus be placed in the most important position possible, which is at the beginning. Thus, in both the headline and the opening paragraph I led off with the bake sale. Since in headlines one tries to be terse, my headline read "PTA BAKE SALE." In the body, to give

it a little flavor, a sense of history, and an additional note of ac-
curacy, I referred to it as the *"Annual* PTA Bake Sale." If it
were a little more significant, say the fiftieth annual bake sale, I
might have added that in the headline, and of course in the opening paragraph as well. Since the opening paragraph should state
all the salient facts, anything I had included in the headline, such
as the date and the school, would also appear in the opening paragraph. But why did I add "in the gymnasium"? Why not "from
9 A.M. to 4 P.M." or "for the benefit of the school's library"?
Basically, I have to admit, for reasons of style. "In the gymnasium" seemed to flow the most smoothly after the initial words,
and "The Sale will begin at 9 A.M." seemed to be a good way to
begin the second paragraph. This, then, is a matter of personal
choice, since all three—the specific area, the time, and the reason
for the sale—are about equally important.

Why, though, do I capitalize Bake Sale in the first paragraph,
and also capitalize Sale in the second paragraph? Couldn't they
just as easily (and perhaps even more correctly) be written with
lower-case letters? Certainly they could, but they wouldn't look as
important. Anything capitalized always assumes more importance, and since what you're trying to do is stress the importance
of this event, and since the words seem to transpose into capitali-
zation without any undue strain, the wise thing to do is capitalize
them.

In the second paragraph I include all the rest of the essentials
—the time of the sale and the reason for the sale. The fact that
the pastries will be furnished by the schoolchildren's parents is
less essential, but adds a little human interest to the story.

The final paragraph in this case is tertiary in interest and,
really, just not that important. However, it does give the mothers
in charge their due, perhaps saves them a few phone calls in en-
listing a few more bakers or money-takers, and, finally, rounds out
the release.

Just to show that a release can be written in a variety of ways
and still be right, let me try this one again. You'll note that a few
things remain unchanged, though.

FROM: WILUDA MEYER
        123 Graceful Lane
        Jacksonville, Alabama 36265
        (205) 555-1212

FOR IMMEDIATE RELEASE, PLEASE

PTA BAKE SALE TO BE HELD MAY 4TH AT JACKSON-VILLE ELEMENTARY SCHOOL

The Annual PTA Bake Sale will be held on May 4th at Jacksonville Elementary School, running from 9 A.M. to 4 P.M., for the benefit of the school's library.

The Sale, which will take place in the gymnasium, will offer cakes, pies, and cookies, furnished by the parents of the school's pupils. In charge of the event are PTA members Orvaline Wynette, Jane Smith, and Wiluda Meyer, who announce that they are interested in hearing from anyone who would like to help out with the Sale. Those who wish to do so may contact them through the school.

Proceeds of the Sale will go toward buying books and supplies for the library.

Let's try another one. Say you're an author, you're going to have a book published, would like people to find out about it, and have a feeling your publisher's not going to be too helpful in that direction. What to do? Well, you can publicize it yourself, and that's what this book is all about.

However, to publicize yourself might seem a little too self-serving. It might bother the people you're going after, and it might bother you. My suggestion—although you certainly can try doing it yourself, and some people are their own best salesmen—is that you have a friend or relative stand in for you as your publicist. You can write the releases, you can send them out, you can even go after people via the phone, but it might make things just a bit easier for you if you don't appear to be the one tooting your own horn. Just be sure, if it does go out under your cousin Velna's name, that she knows enough about you and your book to be able to talk about it with a reasonable amount of knowledge should an editor or talent-booker call.

Let's suppose your name is Art John and you've written a novel called *War and Puce,* about an interior decorator's adventures in the South Pacific in 1944, based to some extent on your own experiences. This is your first book, to be published September 10 by Bradbury and Son at a price of $12.95, and for most of your life you have been a copywriter at the Scrooge and Schweitzer advertising agency. The first thing you want to do is let people know the book is going to come out. First you've got to write a release that is appropriate for your local newspaper. And let's say you enlist a girlfriend, Bambi Dole, to stand in for you as your press agent. Here's how your initial release might read in your campaign for attention:

FROM: BAMBI DOLE
           777 Brooklyn Avenue
           Brooklyn, New York 11220
           (212) 555-1212

<u>FOR IMMEDIATE RELEASE, PLEASE</u>

<u>"WAR AND PUCE," FIRST NOVEL BY FLATBUSH'S ART JOHN, TO BE PUBLISHED SEPTEMBER 10TH</u>

"War and Puce," a first novel by Flatbush author Art John, will be published September 10th by Bradbury and Son. ($12.95)

A novel about an interior decorator's adventures in the South Pacific in 1944, "War and Puce" has been based to some extent on the author's own experiences. Currently a copywriter at the Scrooge and Schweitzer advertising agency, Mr. John resides at 453 Lenox Road, and is a graduate of Flatbush's P.S. 235

and Erasmus Hall High School with a B.A. from Brooklyn College and an M.A. from Oxford University.

That's it, folks. Did you notice? No third paragraph. That's because in this case there's no need for one. And now let's break down this release as we did the first.

You've got a three-way choice for starting off your headline. Is the name of the novel most important to you, is the fact that it's a novel most important, or is your own name most important to you? It's really your choice here; you can kick off with any of them. Since it's a first novel, which makes it (if I'm not being redundant) more singular, it's important that this is stressed in the headline. And of course it's essential, as always, to get in the date. Then the editor will know when to run the release, and the reader will know when the book will be available.

The first paragraph echoes the headline, and adds the secondary information about the publisher and the price of the book. (Of course, if you feel it absolutely essential that people also know who the publisher is, you should add it to the headline—you've got the room.) The reason the price is quoted is that book prices are always quoted in releases, and you want to make your release look professional.

The second paragraph deals with the secondary news: what the book is about, and just why the author should be of interest to people who read a newspaper devoted to news of the area.

Now here's an example of a single-paragraph release. There are certain publications that list the impending publication of books (the *New York Times* is one). They may list only the title of the book, the author's name, a brief description of the book, the publisher, and the price. So your release should read this way:

FROM: BAMBI DOLE
             777 Brooklyn Avenue
             Brooklyn, New York 11220
             (212) 555-1212

<u>FOR IMMEDIATE RELEASE, PLEASE</u>

<u>"WAR AND PUCE," BY ART JOHN, TO BE PUBLISHED
SEPTEMBER 10TH BY BRADBURY AND SON.</u>

"War and Puce," a first novel by Art John, about an interior
decorator's World War II adventures, will be published on
September 10th by Bradbury and Son. Price will be $12.95.

In this case, all that's been added in the body of the release is
the fact that it's a first novel (expendable, I admit, but I like
the feeling of singularity it adds—perhaps the book space on that
day won't permit the listing of all books to be published on September 10 and this may give it a slight edge) and the price. Your
choice here would be to drop the word "first" and simply write the
price as in the first example: "($12.95)." Otherwise, everything
should remain constant.

All right, Mr. Author, you've got your mention in the local
paper, and the listing in all the publications you could track down
that list new books. It's time, you think, for bigger game. The
daily paper, the local radio and TV shows, or, for that matter, the
newspaper and radio and TV shows of any other localities you
plan to visit. How should your release read?

If it's a newspaper that covers your locality, do mention, as
before, where you're from. In every other respect, though, your
release should read something like this:

FROM: BAMBI DOLE
         777 Brooklyn Avenue
         Brooklyn, New York 11220
         (212) 555-1212

<u>FOR IMMEDIATE RELEASE, PLEASE</u>

<u>"WAR AND PUCE," FIERY WAR NOVEL BY NEW
WRITER ART JOHN, TO BE PUBLISHED SEPTEMBER
10TH BY BRADBURY AND SON.</u>

"War and Puce," described as one man's attempt to reconcile the meaning of life, death, and interior decorating against a background of savage warfare, will be published September 10th by Bradbury and Son. ($12.95)

This first novel, written by advertising copywriter Art John, is based to some extent on the writer's personal experiences during the Second World War. The author was stationed in Fort Dix, New Jersey, in 1944 and 1945, and one of his functions was to review war news as it arrived from overseas and present it in a digested form to his company commander. Mr. John's fascinating decorating experiences, which were cut short when it became evident that he could not make a proper Windsor knot, were also drawn upon in the writing of the book.

Beau Blotchner, the Private First Class who dominates "War and Puce," is a man who suddenly finds his private universe shattered by a world cataclysm and inferior digital coordination. His attempt to bridge the gap between the ideal and the too real, told through interior monologues and eye-shielding loveplay with the book's other major character, Bambi Dohl, makes up a saga of monumental proportions, throbbing with a Gargantuan appetite for life, love, and pastel hues.

Well, I can't wait to read it, let alone book you on my talk show. But seriously, folks . . . what did we do here, and why?

This release is your big gun, the one you hope to sell yourself with. This is a release you're sending out not only to newspapers, wire services, and syndicates in the hope they'll run it, but also to places that may decide to do feature interviews on you—newspapers, wire services, syndicates, magazines, trade journals (magazines for soldiers, veterans, interior decorators, whatever you can find that makes sense), radio and television shows, book critics.

Therefore, this release should include absolutely everything that will interest the reader and make him consider that not only would it be important to print the release, but that it might make sense to consider the author for an interview. Or, in the case of a book critic, whet his appetite for the book. The sad state of affairs in the book world is that, of the around forty thousand new titles printed every year, only about half get reviewed, and many of those by only one or two obscure critics. So if you can get a critic interested ahead of time, you're way ahead of the game.

On this release, you've been lucky. In all likelihood you have seen the jacket copy for the book, and you've been able to pluck most of it straight from the jacket and set it down plump in the middle of your release. You'll notice that the verbiage in this release is considerably more colorful than what we've seen so far. That's because of two things. One is that you're dealing in an area that allows for expressiveness, and the second is that when you're in an area that allows for expressiveness, as a press agent you should take full advantage of it.

If you feel your book is fiery, or have heard or seen it described that way, don't be shy about calling it that. Whatever seems most important about the book is what you should say about it, in terms as pungent (without being florid) as you can find. The general theme of the book should be touched on, its era, place, and a basic sense of the plot, without getting into the plot's details. Your best guide here is looking not only at your own book jacket, but at the jackets of other books similar to yours. The writing inside the book jacket is designed to sell the book, and therefore its general style, often its exact style, is absolutely right for the basics of a book's news release.

One note of caution on a point that will be touched on later: If you're going to use this release to help you grab some feature interviews in the press or on the air, it is best to first call (better yet, have Bambi do it, if she's willing and able), explain what you're calling about, and then, if there's any interest, send the release with a covering note or letter, plus, if at all possible, a biography of yourself. (Don't worry—we'll explain all about biographies later.)

Disk jockeys have special problems. They're very much in

front of the public, which is good, but so are all their fellow disk jockeys, which is bad. Furthermore, in a business that depends on ratings, a disk jockey with low ratings is in terrible trouble, because out there are a lot of other disk jockeys with very good credentials, maybe better than yours, looking for jobs. What to do?

Well, of course, the first thing to do is to try to be the very best in the business. The next, and here's where publicity comes in, is to let even more people know about you, on the chance they'll be intrigued enough to tune you in or, having stumbled on you, think, "Oh, yeah, that's Mumbles Branigan, I've heard about him," and leave the dial where it is so they can find out exactly who this Mumbles Branigan they've read about is.

The first thing to do when you've just started your job, or, even better, when you know you're going to be starting your job, is to get out a release about it. Sometimes the radio station will do that, but sometimes it won't. And when it won't—well, maybe it'll at least let you use its stationery and the name of whoever handles publicity for it.

FROM: JULIA ADULT
         15 Swann's Way
         Kiowa, Iowa 50101
         (319) 555-1212

FOR IMMEDIATE RELEASE, PLEASE

MUMBLES BRANIGAN, "THE DEAN OF THE SCENE,"
TO JOIN KAWA JULY 10TH IN MORNING SLOT

Mumbles Branigan, self-described "Dean of the Scene," will begin a three-hour daily radio show on KAWA July 10th, playing the best in rock and chamber music from 9 A.M. till noon.

Branigan, a native of Pebbles, Oregon, most recently had his own rock-chamber show at station WDNC in Hollywood,

Oklahoma. Previous to that, he served as staff announcer at WHAT in Sternum, Florida.

Branigan replaces Roderick "Unjowah" Featherstone-Haugh, who has left KAWA to devote himself to personal projects.

Just a few notes here. If you're going to begin the show soon, the headline and body should read "MONDAY, JULY 10TH." If it's going to be the Monday coming up, then both headline and body should read, "THIS MONDAY (JULY 10TH)." This is simply to make the whole thing clearer to whoever's reading and (let's hope) using your release. It's not strictly necessary to inject Featherstone-Haugh's name here, but it does give the story a sense of continuity. Naturally, you should check with Featherstone-Haugh to find out what he wants said.

All right, you're now installed at KAWA and you find yourself being asked to make personal appearances around town. Maybe you get paid, maybe you do it just to get closer to your fans; in any event, here you have an opportunity to get some more publicity. Perhaps the station draws a line at sending out releases on this, so you've got to go off again and do it yourself. Again you've got your choice of sending it out under your own name or having a friend stand in for you. In any case, the resultant release should look something like this, given the information that you'll be appearing at a "Discotheque Night" at St. Matthew's Church in Hinsdale, on Friday, May 6, beginning at 8:00 P.M., and you've clinched the deal a week before you'll be appearing.

FROM: JULIA ADULT
          15 Swann's Way
          Kiowa, Iowa 50101
          (319) 555-1212

<u>FOR IMMEDIATE RELEASE, PLEASE</u>

<u>KAWA'S MUMBLES BRANIGAN TO HEADLINE "DIS-COTHEQUE NIGHT" AT ST. MATTHEW'S CHURCH, HINSDALE, THIS FRIDAY (MAY 6TH).</u>

Mumbles Branigan, who has his own daily morning show here on radio station KAWA, will appear in person at a "Discotheque Night" at St. Matthew's Church in Hinsdale, this Friday evening (May 6th).

Branigan, known to his listeners as "The Dean of the Scene," will serve as master of ceremonies for the evening, as well as "disk jockey" for the records to be played.

The festivities will begin at 8 P.M. St. Matthew's Church is on Main Street in Hinsdale, two blocks north of the Hinsdale-Kiowa intersection. Tickets at the door are $1.50 per person.

Now, all you really care about is getting your name in, Branigan, being the kind of person you are. But you'll be much more sure of getting your release printed if all the essential facts are included in your release. Leave out some, and the editor may wonder what time the affair will begin, may have forgotten (or never known) where the church is located, may feel his readers should know the price of tickets. Without that information, he may be inclined not to print that release. Or even if he wants to, and decides to call Miss Adult for the additional information, he may not get around to it, or perhaps she'll be out when he calls. So always, always include all pertinent information in a release of this kind.

Suppose you've been put in charge of publicity for a cooperative summer day camp in the suburbs, run by the parents themselves. You're told they want a release sent out with information about the opening of the camp. There'll be more releases later on, but this is the first, and is basically to alert people to the fact that the camp will open again a month or two from now. The facts are these: This will be the camp's seventh year in operation, it is a non-profit cooperative camp, run by the mothers of the campers, it's located on the grounds of the local Yeshiva, and is open to all races and creeds, for children aged three to five. The hours will be from ten to two, five days a week, and there will be bus pick-up service. Millicent Pulch is this year's President. Your name is Daisy Bell. See what you can come up with, and then check it out against the following:

FROM: DAISY BELL
        23 Carolin Road
        Sayville, Long Island 11782
        (516) 555-1212

<u>FOR IMMEDIATE RELEASE, PLEASE</u>

<u>SAYVILLE COOPERATIVE DAY CAMP TO REOPEN FOR
SEVENTH SEASON JULY 5TH</u>

The Sayville Cooperative Day Camp, a non-sectarian camp for children aged three to five, will begin its seventh season on July 5th. Parents interested in registering their children for the camp are requested to contact Millicent Pulch, President of the Camp, at 555-1212.

The Camp, which is located on the grounds of the Sayville Yeshiva, is a non-profit Camp run by the mothers of the campers. All normal camp activities are included, and all the mothers participate to some extent in the functioning of the camp.

This year's hours will run from 10 A.M. to 2 P.M., Monday through Friday, and children will be picked up at their homes by bus.

I think this release is pretty self-explanatory. It gives the basic information about the camp, which at this point seems to be all that is needed.

However, what if July 5 is fast approaching and the mothers find there will not be enough campers to make the camp economically feasible? Time now to get out a release that makes the whole venture a little more attractive. And why didn't we write a release like this in the first place? Because no one, from past experience, thought it would be necessary. Why oversell when there's no need?

Now, of course, you need a little more information. But, basically, you can send out pretty much the same release again. Because the news now can be that instead of opening July 5, the camp (because you're sending this second release out at the end of June) is opening next week. See? With a little rewriting, it's news all over again.

FROM: DAISY BELL
           23 Carolin Road
           Sayville, Long Island 11782
           (516) 555-1212

FOR IMMEDIATE RELEASE, PLEASE

SAYVILLE COOPERATIVE DAY CAMP TO REOPEN NEXT WEEK (TUESDAY, JULY 5TH) FOR SEVENTH SEASON: OPENINGS STILL AVAILABLE.

The Sayville Cooperative Day Camp, which will reopen for its seventh season next week (Tuesday, July 5th), announces that a few openings are still available for campers between the ages of 3 and 5.

The Camp, which features home pick-up bus service, is open from 10 A.M. to 2 P.M. Monday through Friday. Camp facilities include a large wading pool, swings, seesaw, recreational and craft activities, with guidance by professional counselors.

Those interested in registering for the camp are requested to call the Camp's President, Millicent Pulch, at 555-1212.

Okay, this time notice not only what we put in, but what we left out, which can be just as important in a release. Obviously, if your release is being sent out with the idea of getting more children to register for your camp, you want to get the fact into the headline and the first paragraph. Since home pick-up service is an attractive feature (the mothers don't have to shlep the kids to the camp themselves), it's a good idea to lead off the second paragraph with this, as well as with the hours. ("Bruno will be out of my hair from ten A.M. to two P.M.? Thank God! Now what is that wonderful woman's phone number?") The wading pool, etc., give a feeling of what the camp is like (just the kind of stuff kids love), and the fact that there will be professional counselors is reassuring.

Did you notice what I left out? Okay, maybe it's a bit Machiavellian, but why not wait till the parents are more sold (i.e., on the phone) before you spring the news that they're going to have to do a little work themselves?

Now suppose you're an actor, and you're out in Hollywood, and you've just landed a small role in a play in Los Angeles. You've been told a release has been sent out, but your name didn't appear in the *Hollywood Reporter* or *Variety,* or any of the local papers. What to do? First of all, like our author friend above, you could have someone send out the release for you. But a certain amount of eccentricity is allowed entertainers, and it's possible you might beguile more editors than you'd turn off if you sent the news out under your own name. Want to take a chance? Okay. Now remember, it's a small role so don't go overboard.

FROM: BARRY MOORE
            1118½ La Sagne Boulevard
            Hollywood, California 90028
            (213) 555-1212

                    FOR IMMEDIATE RELEASE, PLEASE

BARRY MOORE SIGNED FOR ROLE IN "GONEFF WITH THE WIND," OPENING MAY 6TH AT POPLAR THEATRE.

Barry Moore has been signed for the role of Beanman in the Ranild Stekitee play "Goneff with the Wind," which opens May 6th at Sherman Oaks' Poplar Theatre.

Mr. Moore was last seen locally as the corpse in "As You Love it," also at the Poplar.

Now suppose you, Mr. Moore, decide you want to tackle some of the local talk shows. The odds are certainly against you with all those high-priced performers out there, most of them with personal press agents, but why not give it a whirl? You can't lose anything but a little time, and as long as it doesn't cut into your auditioning and your hair-combing, you won't be losing much of anything and you could be gaining quite a bit. One good talk show could land you a role, by implanting your name and personality in a producer's head. Or it could lead you to another talk show, or at the very least make you a little less nervous about doing another one when the opportunity comes up.

What you've got to do is figure out an angle that will make you attractive to the people who book interview shows. Newsiness is best, but sometimes an offbeat, colorful approach can turn the trick for you. Let's try both. And in each case remember that along with the release should go a biography (or bio, as it's known in the trade), unless, of course, your release is worded so that it contains your biography.

Let's say that you use yoga as a way of concentrating your energies as an actor. This could be your angle, just as the fact that of the eight plays you've appeared in, you've been killed in six, or the fact that you studied directly under Lee Strasberg at the Actors Studio in both New York and California, or that you began acting professionally at the age of seven could be an angle. What I'm trying to say is that usually there is some kind of news angle in a person's professional life, and if you dig around enough, you'll find it.

Now, anything colorful or interesting about you personally? Probably, if you think hard enough about it. Let's say you collect toy soldiers of the Napoleonic Era.

FROM: **BARRY MOORE**
1118½ La Sagne Boulevard
Hollywood, California 90028
(213) 555-1212

FOR IMMEDIATE RELEASE, PLEASE

BARRY MOORE SIGNED TO PLAY BEANMAN IN "GONEFF WITH THE WIND": ACTOR SPECIALIZING IN DEATH SCENES WITH SIX IN PAST EIGHT APPEARANCES.

Barry Moore, last seen locally as the corpse in the Poplar Theatre production of "As You Love It," will bite the dust again in his next show, "Goneff with the Wind," which opens May 6th at the Poplar Theatre in Sherman Oaks.

In six of his last eight plays, Moore has been bludgeoned to death, poisoned, throttled, twice died of natural causes, and twice committed suicide, once by hanging and once by being impertinent (to a Southern sheriff). In "Goneff with the Wind," as Beanman, he will cast off this mortal coil when he is, during a power shortage, strapped to a battery-powered electric chair.

Moore, who owns one of the world's finest collections of Napoleonic Era toy soldiers, will go into rehearsal with the play on May 4th.

I think the release is self-explanatory. What I want to remind you of is that if you are going to go after a talk show, call first, conversationally giving the talent-booker the gist of the release, and then, if he expresses interest, send it to him along with a note and a bio.

Suppose you've decided to open an art gallery, or a grocery store, or a boutique. It's a strictly commercial enterprise. Would a newspaper print such a story? Why not? Theaters are commercial enterprises, and they're in the newspaper all the time. Admittedly, a grocery store has not quite the cachet a theatrical attraction has, but why not take a shot at it? Herewith, releases on three new businesses:

FROM: REMBRANDT KEANE
           73 Ochre Way
           Dalton, Massachusetts 01007
           (413) 555-1212

FOR IMMEDIATE RELEASE, PLEASE

NEW ART GALLERY, WE WERE FRAMED, TO OPEN HERE DECEMBER 10TH ON GRUNGE ROAD.

Dalton's newest art gallery, We Were Framed, will open on December 10th at 122 Grunge Road, under the ownership and management of Henrietta Klahd and her husband, Clark Klahd.

The shop, formerly Ralph's Pizzeria, will feature original oil paintings, water colors, etchings, and sculpture, as well as prints and silk screen reproductions. A framing service will also be an important adjunct of the shop.

Hours will be from 9 A.M. to 9 P.M., Monday through Saturday.

Self-explanatory, I think, but to get a little more attention and perhaps ensure your receiving space with your release, you might decide to have a gala opening. Wine, cheese, and artists seem to go nicely together, so why not a free glass of wine and a bit of cheese to everyone who visits the shop the first day? This could be your first release, or a second release to follow the one above. Let's say it's the latter and the opening is just a week away. Because of this we'll say "this Monday," with the date in parentheses.

FROM: REMBRANDT KEANE
         73 Ochre Way
         Dalton, Massachusetts 01007
         (413) 555-1212

FOR IMMEDIATE RELEASE, PLEASE

NEW ART GALLERY, WE WERE FRAMED, TO OFFER FREE WINE AND CHEESE AT GALA OPENING HERE THIS MONDAY (DECEMBER 10TH), ON GRUNGE ROAD.

Free wine and cheese will be offered to all customers who attend the gala opening of Dalton's newest art gallery, We Were Framed, when it opens this Monday, December 10th.

Located at 122 Grunge Road, We Were Framed will feature original oil paintings, water colors, etchings, and sculpture, as well as prints and silk screen reproductions, under the direction and ownership of Henrietta Klahd and her husband, Clark Klahd. In addition, the shop will offer a framing service.

We Were Framed will be open Monday through Saturday from 9 A.M. to 9 P.M.

The only thing I'd like to add here is that if the shop has particularly valuable paintings and/or sculpture by any noted artists or locally famed artists, they could be described in this release or the one above, in as much detail as seems warranted. It would make the release more newsy.

Now here's a try at letting people know you're about to open a new grocery store. Or, just to vary the situation and show you how to handle something after the fact, let's assume you were too busy to publicize the event in front, or just plain forgot about it. Here's how it should read:

FROM: JOE MELLON
         25 Temple Road
         Orange, New Jersey 07050
         (201) 555-1212

FOR IMMEDIATE RELEASE, PLEASE

MELLON'S GROCERY CELEBRATING GALA OPENING:
TO FEATURE GOURMET CORNER.

Mellon's Grocery is Orange's newest grocery store, having opened here recently at 25 Temple Road.

Owned and operated by Mr. and Mrs. Joseph Mellon, Mellon's plans to provide Orange with the freshest in farm produce, as well as a wide variety of frozen and canned foods. A unique feature of the store is its Gourmet Corner, which specializes in exotic foods and spices, many of them imported.

Mellon's is open from 7 A.M. to midnight Monday through Saturday, and from 9 A.M. till noon on Sunday.

Simple enough. Now you may not have a Gourmet Corner, but it's quite possible you'll have something else—home delivery, locally grown vegetables, etc., that you can spotlight to make your store sound different from all the rest.

Ready to open that boutique? Clothes are not one of my strong points, but I'll give it a try. At least the basic form will be right:

FROM: ANGELA FABRIQUE
         22 Hehm Boulevard
         Lacy, North Dakota 58457
         (701) 555-1212

FOR IMMEDIATE RELEASE, PLEASE

THE WAGES OF SYNTHETICS, NEW BOUTIQUE, TO
OPEN HERE FEBRUARY 13TH

The Wages of Synthetics, a new boutique specializing in the latest informal fashions, will open here on February 13th at 123 Penney Street.

Betsy Cuite and Veronica Riche, both of them native-born residents, will own and operate the shop. Both Miss Cuite and Miss Riche studied for four years at the Fashion Institute in Fargo. Fashions by such noted names as Masters, Black, and Welles will be featured.

The Wages of Synthetics will be open three days a week, Thursday through Saturday, from 1 P.M. till 7 P.M.

Just one thing I'd like to mention here. You may have noticed that I tend always to refer to the subject of the release by its proper name, rather than a generic. For instance, in the final paragraph, I could have said "The Shop" instead of "The Wages of Synthetics." But since you're trying to sell the subject of your release, the more times you can gracefully fit it in, the better. It may run that many times in its published form, which means the public's mind is being jogged that much more. And if not—well, at least you're making more of an impact on the editor's consciousness, which can be helpful in a future release. The feeling "Oh, yeah, I've heard of that" can make something seem more legitimate, more established, more "real," and thus more worthy of news interest.

Let's take a politician now, and follow him through a series of releases, beginning with his announcement of his intention to run for councilman:

FROM: STEPHEN GATES
        10 Tarrytown Street
        Woods, Washington 98072
        (206) 555-1212

FOR IMMEDIATE RELEASE, PLEASE

STEPHEN GATES TO RUN FOR COUNCILMAN ON INDEPENDENT TICKET.

Stephen Gates, well-known local plumber, announces that he will enter the race for Councilman of Woods as an independent. This will be the first political venture for Mr. Gates, who has lived in Woods for the past five years, and is the father of three children, all of whom attend Woods Grammar School. Mr. Gates is an ardent advocate of a better nutritional program for schoolchildren, and will make that a major issue in the campaign.

The 35-year-old former native of Martense, Missouri, will kick off his campaign with a speech on February 22nd at the Rotary Club on Ellsberg Avenue.

* * *

FROM: STEPHEN GATES
          10 Tarrytown Street
          Woods, Washington 98072
          (206) 555-1212

FOR IMMEDIATE RELEASE, PLEASE

STEPHEN GATES TO MAKE FIRST SPEECH IN CAMPAIGN FOR COUNCILMAN ON MONDAY (FEBRUARY 22ND) AT ROTARY CLUB.

Stephen Gates, who announced his candidacy for the position of town Councilman last week, will make his first speech of the campaign on Monday (February 22nd) at the Rotary Club, at 8 P.M.

A major topic of the speech will be the poor nutrition offered by the lunchroom of Woods Grammar School. Mr. Gates, who has all three of his children enrolled at the school, is planning to make the issue a central theme in his campaign.

The public will be invited to the Rotary Club, which is located on Ellsberg Avenue, near Barker Street.

Okay. Mr. Gates gave his speech, and perhaps some, or even all, of the press didn't attend. In that case, prepared copies of his speech, done as press releases, should go out to the press. If they didn't go out before the speech, it would be wisest to get them to the news desks by hand as soon as the speech has been given. Here's how this release might go:

FROM: STEPHEN GATES
            10 Tarrytown Street
            Woods, Washington, 98072
            (206) 555-1212

<u>FOR IMMEDIATE RELEASE, PLEASE</u>

<u>STEPHEN GATES ATTACKS SCHOOL LUNCHROOM POLICY IN ROTARY CLUB SPEECH: DEMANDS SODA AND SNACK MACHINES BE REMOVED.</u>

Stephen Gates, in his kickoff speech in his campaign for Woods Councilman last night (Monday, February 22nd), said that if elected to office, he would have the soda and snack machines removed from the grammar school lunchroom.

"The money that the schoolchildren should be spending for wholesome sandwiches, hot lunches, and milk is instead being spent on the junk food purveyed by the vending devices installed in Woods Grammar School," Mr. Gates said in a speech at the Rotary Club that was open to the public. "These machines provide no nutritional benefit, in fact are detrimental to the health of the children who buy from them, and, furthermore, provide a profit to private business as well as to the school. If I am elected Councilman," he stated, "I shall do everything in my power to have the machines removed."

Mr. Gates also touched on the issue of noise control, and suggested that he was in favor of banning the use of all power-driven outdoor tools, including lawnmowers and chain saws, after 10 P.M. and before 8 A.M. weekdays, and before 9 A.M. on weekends.

That's the general idea on political releases. If you're about to embark on a campaign of your own, I suggest you get to the local library and read the back issues of your local paper to see how former candidates handled their campaigns. It should furnish you with a number of further ideas, and perhaps also give you a few clues as to what not to do.

We'll come back to Mr. Gates later, but now it's time to give attention to those readers who'll be doing some publicity for a theater group. A theater group lends itself readily to publicity. People are interested in entertainment, and as a result most papers have an Amusements section. Also, a play has a story, an author, a director, a producer, a cast, and behind-the-scenes technicians, most of whom lend themselves to news releases, pictures, column items, and feature interviews.

Let's take a single production, *Wine, Women and Monotones,* by Noel Braveman, given by the Shabbe Players, and get an idea of just how many releases we can send out in advance on one show.

FROM: ENOCH DARDENE
THE SHABBE PLAYERS
22 Aster Street
Slade, Nevada 89430
(702) 555-1212

FOR IMMEDIATE RELEASE, PLEASE

THE SHABBE PLAYERS' NEXT PRODUCTION, "WINE WOMEN AND MONOTONES," BY NOEL BRAVEMAN, TO OPEN AUGUST 12TH, FOR TWO WEEKS.

For their third production of the season, The Shabbe Players will present the first local production of the Noel Braveman drama "Wine, Women and Monotones," beginning August 12th, for two weeks at the Granada Theatre, 123 Hoover Avenue.

"Wine, Women and Monotones," which will feature a cast of fifteen, ran successfully on Broadway in 1953 for 122 performances, and was acclaimed as "timely," "avant garde," and "warmly nostalgic." "Wine, Women and Monotones" is the tender story of the love of a young society girl for a sensitive, poetic ax murderer. Their attempt to separate the artificial gulf between them is a timeless theme, and the resultant drama is considered to be Braveman's finest work.

Pre-production work on the play has already begun, with Arthur Feckless, last seen as Freud in "Madame X," serving for the first time as producer with the Shabbe Players.

* * *

FROM: ENOCH DARDENE
       THE SHABBE PLAYERS
       22 Aster Street
       Slade, Nevada 89430
       (702) 555-1212

FOR IMMEDIATE RELEASE, PLEASE

MARTIN BRANDMAN TO DIRECT "WINE, WOMEN AND MONOTONES," OPENING AUGUST 12TH AT GRANADA THEATRE.

Martin Brandman will direct the third production of the season by the Shabbe Players, the former Broadway stage success, "Wine, Women and Monotones," which will open August 12th at the Granada Theatre.

The Noel Braveman work will be Brandman's first directorial effort with the Shabbe Players, although he has staged a number of productions with various other stock companies, among them "The Sound of Mujik," a story of the Russian Revolution, which had a pre-Broadway tryout tour two years ago in Wyoming and Idaho.

Brandman is currently casting the play, which will be produced by Arthur Feckless.

*   *   *

FROM: ENOCH DARDENE
         THE SHABBE PLAYERS
         22 Aster Street
         Slade, Nevada 89430
         (702) 555-1212

FOR IMMEDIATE RELEASE, PLEASE

SALLY FORBES TO PLAY LEAD ROLE IN "WINE, WOMEN AND MONOTONES," OPENING AUGUST 12TH AT GRANADA THEATRE.

Sally Forbes, last seen with the Shabbe Players as Trock in their all-female version of "Winterset," will have the leading feminine role in Noel Braveman's dramatic hit "Wine, Women and Monotones" when it opens at the Granada Theatre August 12th, for two weeks.

Miss Forbes will play Artis, the idealistic young society girl who falls in love with an ax murderer, it was announced today by Arthur Feckless, who will produce the former Broadway success, to be seen·for the first time locally. Miss Forbes is in her fifth year with the Shabbe Players, and formerly appeared in several productions at Marsupial High School in Marsupial, Wisconsin.

*   *   *

FROM: ENOCH DARDENE
         THE SHABBE PLAYERS
         22 Aster Street
         Slade, Nevada 89430
         (702) 555-1212

<u>FOR IMMEDIATE RELEASE, PLEASE</u>

<u>BENTLEY DIFFIDENT TO PLAY POETIC AX MUR-</u>
<u>DERER IN "WINE, WOMEN AND MONOTONES," SHABBE</u>
<u>PLAYERS' AUGUST 12–25 PRODUCTION.</u>

Bentley Diffident, who starred in the Shabbe Players' last production, "A Story of Two Cities," will also take the lead male role in the first local presentation of the Broadway hit "Wine, Women and Monotones," by Noel Braveman.

Diffident will play Hugo Igor, a sensitive, though brutal, ax murderer. Appearing opposite him as a naive society girl will be Sally Forbes. Diffident has previously been seen here in "A Tale of Two Suburbs" and "Hamlets: Two."

"Wine, Women and Monotones" will be the third production of the season by the Shabbe Players, and will open on August 12th for two weeks at the Granada Theatre, under the direction of Martin Brandman, and the producing aegis of Arthur Feckless.

*   *   *

FROM: ENOCH DARDENE
         THE SHABBE PLAYERS
         22 Aster Street
         Slade, Nevada 89430
         (702) 555-1212

FOR IMMEDIATE RELEASE, PLEASE

FEATURE ROLES CAST FOR "WINE, WOMEN AND MONOTONES," OPENING AUGUST 12TH AT GRANADA THEATRE FOR TWO WEEKS.

Director Martin Brandman has cast the six feature roles in Noel Braveman's "Wine, Women and Monotones," the Shabbe Players production opening August 12th at the Granada Theatre for a fortnight.

Selected to support Sally Forbes and Bentley Diffident, who will play the lead roles, are Johnny Mack Sepia, Stella Houston, Joan Crayfish, George C. Hibernian, Cary Lee, and Robert Redbug. Mr. Sepia will appear as Oscar Noovau, Miss Houston as Jane, the landlady, and Miss Crayfish as the bubbly Mrs. Kohla, while Mr. Hibernian, Mr. Lee, and Mr. Redbug will play the fish merchants.

Direction will be by Martin Brandman, and the production will be helmed by Arthur Feckless.

* * *

FROM: ENOCH DARDENE
        THE SHABBE PLAYERS
        22 Aster Street
        Slade, Nevada 89430
        (702) 555-1212

FOR IMMEDIATE RELEASE, PLEASE

CASTING COMPLETED FOR "WINE, WOMEN AND MONOTONES," NEW SHABBE PLAYERS PRODUCTION TO OPEN AUGUST 12TH AT GRANADA THEATRE FOR TWO WEEKS.

Director Martin Brandman has completed casting of the Noel Braveman drama "Wine, Women and Monotones," announces producer Arthur Feckless.

Joining the previously announced Shabbe Players cast of Sally Forbes, Bentley Diffident, Johnny Mack Sepia, Stella Houston, Joan Crayfish, George C. Hibernian, Cary Lee, and Robert Redbug will be Shabbe Players company members Betty Lee, Dorothy Laless, Steve McKing, Micheline Gide, Abraham Mercury, Basil Rathgrape, and Shirley Navel.

"Wine, Women and Monotones" was one of the hits of the 1953 Broadway dramatic season, and will open August 12th at the Granada Theatre for a two-week run.

* * *

FROM: ENOCH DARDENE
           THE SHABBE PLAYERS
           22 Aster Street
           Slade, Nevada 89430
           (702) 555-1212

FOR IMMEDIATE RELEASE, PLEASE

REHEARSALS BEGIN AUGUST 2ND FOR "WINE, WOMEN AND MONOTONES," OPENING AUGUST 12TH FOR TWO WEEKS.

Rehearsals will get under way on August 2nd for the third production of the season by the Shabbe Players, Noel Braveman's "Wine, Women and Monotones." Sally Forbes and Bentley Diffident will star in the roles of the star-crossed lovers, under the direction of Martin Brandman. Arthur Feckless will produce.

The former Broadway hit premieres August 12th at the Granada Theatre for two weeks.

* * *

FROM: ENOCH DARDENE
           THE SHABBE PLAYERS

22 Aster Street
Slade, Nevada 89430
(702) 555-1212

FOR IMMEDIATE RELEASE, PLEASE

ARCH REMARQUE, MADELINE PROUST, DRYDEN MAR-
TINI TO CREATE LIGHTING, COSTUMES, SETS FOR
"WINE, WOMEN AND MONOTONES" OPENING AUGUST
12TH.

Lighting expert Arch Remarque, costume designer Madeline
Proust, and set designer Dryden Martini, who have contributed
so heavily to previous productions by the Shabbe Players, will
again work their wonders for the local theatre group in its next
production, Noel Braveman's "Wine, Women and Monotones,"
opening August 12th at the Granada Theatre.

Just a breather here before we continue. This gives you an idea
as to how far you can go with pre-production releases. Obviously,
some of these can be broken down into even more releases and it
wouldn't take much inventiveness to come up with still more.
Notice that the name of the show, the date of its opening, and the
name of the theater are constantly stressed. Also, the main
talents involved are almost always mentioned, partly because it's
important that potential ticket-buyers know they will be doing the
show, and partly because, if they're temperamental or ultra-sensi-
tive, seeing a release go out without their names could result in a
less pleasant life for everyone concerned. In the last release I
left out director, producer, and stars because they're really unnecessary and at this point everyone's been mentioned enough.
But if I were in the actual situation of sending out that release, it's
quite likely I'd prefer discretion to succinctness, and would throw
in all four names.

In addition to the signings releases, there are two more releases, sometimes known as "readers," which we can send out before the opening. These releases are more like feature stories and, in fact, tell the story of the playwright and the play. They can run as long as two pages, double-spaced. However, since they may be cut by the paper, it's a good idea to get your salient facts in near the beginning. By the by, another release on plays, which often goes out but which I haven't done here, is a release on ticket prices, and the prices may be incorporated into other releases. Since this production is the third of the season, it's assumed that people know your price range, and only in the final release would I see any need to include prices.

FROM: ENOCH DARDENE
          THE SHABBE PLAYERS
          22 Aster Street
          Slade, Nevada 89430
          (702) 555-1212

FOR IMMEDIATE RELEASE, PLEASE

NOEL BRAVEMAN, A MASTER OF DRAMA: HIS "WINE, WOMEN AND MONOTONES" TO OPEN AUGUST 12TH IN SHABBE PLAYERS PRODUCTION.

Among those who know theatre, many agree that Noel Braveman, whose dramatic hit "Wine, Women and Monotones" will open here August 12th, at the Granada Theatre, was a master of the dramatic form.

Braveman's play, starring Sally Forbes and Bentley Diffident, will be seen for the first time locally in its two-week engagement by the Shabbe Players, and should be of interest to all followers of theatre, since it is a finely crafted work that engages all the emotions in its depiction of the love of two young people in a world only partly of their making.

Braveman was born in 1915 in Snell, Mississippi, and after

twelve years of schooling, became a newspaperman, working for a time as the police reporter in Lubbock, New Hampshire. Desiring what he called at the time "a chance to expand," Braveman decided to move to New York and make his way there as a writer.

He tried his hand first as an author, but his two novels, "Just a Guy Called Pop" and "Mom: A Woman," were not successful, and in 1938, after being invalided out of the U.S. Army with a sick headache, Braveman wrote the first of his Broadway plays, "The Story of Man and God and Life," written in free verse and performed without scenery or props or, eventually, actors, as it was not a success.

"Wine, Women and Monotones" was Braveman's next Main Stem venture, and created a success that he never quite repeated. Eventually, Braveman turned his attention to poetry, but in his last years he spent most of his time gardening, occasionally in his own garden.

In his personal life, Braveman was known in 1943 as quite a man about town, often making headlines with his wild parties. He died in 1957, shortly after an unsuccessful revival of "Wine, Women and Monotones."

"Wine, Women and Monotones" will feature a cast of fifteen when it begins its two-week run here, and will be directed by Martin Brandman, and produced by Arthur Feckless.

* * *

FROM: ENOCH DARDENE
         THE SHABBE PLAYERS
         22 Aster Street
         Slade, Nevada 89430
         (702) 555-1212

FOR IMMEDIATE RELEASE, PLEASE

"WINE, WOMEN AND MONOTONES" A STUDY IN EMOTIONAL TURMOIL: OPENS HERE AUGUST 12TH AT GRANADA THEATRE.

Noel Braveman's "Wine, Women and Monotones," which opens here August 12th in the Shabbe Players' third production of the season, was called "timely," "avant garde," and "warmly nostalgic" when it lit up Broadway for 122 performances in 1953. It was also called "the most singularly emotional dramatic experience of the past three months."

Emotion is the dominant theme of "Wine, Women and Monotones." Although the love of a young society girl for a brutal ax murderer is no longer as fresh a subject as it was in 1953, Braveman's penetrating way with his typewriter has captured emotions as fresh as this morning's jumbo package of enriched white bread.

The play is set in a Park Avenue penthouse occupied by Oscar Noovau (the latter name a clever piece of symbolism by Braveman) and his lovely daughter, Artis. When Hugo Igor, the eccentric but likeable ax murderer, turns up in their apartment, having lost his way on the train ride to the State Penitentiary, Artis finds herself falling hopelessly in love with a man, as she puts it, "old enough to be my husband."

Complications swiftly follow, since Oscar Noovau is steadfastly opposed to her relationship with "this young roughneck," as he so tellingly phrases it. His daughter attempts to win him over by going on a hunger strike, but Noovau hires scabs who feed her intravenously.

The introduction of a lonely landlady and three deep-thinking fish merchants suddenly complicates the situation, and by the second act, despair seems the lot of all, although the fish merchants cheer up noticeably when they realize that the next day is Friday.

The final act of "Wine, Women and Monotones" is a Broadway legend, and it is not our place here to spoil an evening's entertainment by disclosing it. Suffice it to say that this third and last act has been compared to the thrilling climax of Ian Plebe's classic "The Story of P.S. 109."

When "Wine, Women and Monotones" opens at the Granada Theatre for its two-week run, produced by Arthur Feckless, and directed by Martin Brandman, Artis Noovau will be played by Sally Forbes, and Hugo Igor by Bentley Diffident, with thirteen others completing the cast of fifteen.

And now here is the last pre-opening release:

FROM: ENOCH DARDENE
         THE SHABBE PLAYERS
         22 Aster Street
         Slade, Nevada 89430
         (702) 555-1212

FOR IMMEDIATE RELEASE, PLEASE

"WINE, WOMEN AND MONOTONES," PERFORMED BY SHABBE PLAYERS, TO OPEN WEDNESDAY (AUGUST 12TH) AT GRANADA THEATRE, FOR TWO WEEKS.

Noel Braveman's Broadway hit "Wine, Women and Monotones" will be presented for the first time locally beginning Wednesday (August 12th), in a two-week engagement at the Granada Theatre, 22 Aster Street.

Starring in the long-run dramatic smash will be Sally Forbes and Bentley Diffident as the lovers, with Johnny Mack Sepia, Stella Houston, Joan Crayfish, George C. Hibernian, Cary Lee, and Robert Redbug featured among the cast of fifteen, in a play that emotionally explores the plight of a young society girl and a sensitive young ax murderer as they fall helplessly in love.

The production, directed by Martin Brandman and produced by Arthur Feckless, will have lighting by Arch Remarque, costumes by Madeline Proust, and sets by Dryden ("Ted") Martini. Curtain time will be at 8:30, with ticket prices ranging from $2.50 to $2.25.

Actually, that is not quite the last release. A release known as an "Opening Tonight" release should go out three days before the opening. This is an abbreviated release, with the only major change being that instead of saying the play opens Wednesday, August 12th, you write, "OPENS TONIGHT (WEDNESDAY, AUGUST 12TH)," in both headline and body of the release.

Finally, although this is not exactly a release, you will find it a good idea to type up a page similar to a theatrical playbill, listing the actors in the order of their appearance, and the parts they play, as well as other production credits (director, producer, set designer, etc.), and send several copies to the drama desk of any newspaper that covers, so that the critic can have it at hand while typing his review, and the Drama Editor can set it alongside the review.

*   *   *

Sometimes you send out a press release that you don't expect to run anywhere. There is a release you send out to alert the news desks of newspapers, radio and TV stations, wire services, syndicates, magazines, and trade journals that there will be a news event that merits coverage.

This release should be as short and to the point as possible, so that a busy editor can take it all in at a glance. If he can't, there's an excellent chance he'll discard it, so be careful about this. The five W's apply even more certainly here, so keep them in mind whenever you write one of these.

There is no specific form for one of these releases, but I've found the following, with a paragraph or two on the event itself, followed by an at-your-fingertips summary, to be effective:

FROM: ACHILLES POPEINE
           123 Nichols Street
           Foxcroft, Maine 71040
           (207) 555-1212

ATTENTION: NEWS DESKS

EARLY OR LATE SPRING? WINTHROP'S PHARMACY TO HAVE GROUNDHOG MAKE PREDICTION IN "CAVE" THIS MONDAY (FEBRUARY 2ND), GROUNDHOG DAY, AT 11 A.M.

Winthrop's Pharmacy on Main Street, always interested in doing what it can to serve the needs of the population of Foxcroft, will have a live groundhog on its premises on Groundhog Day (this Monday, February 2nd), to see whether we will be greeted with an early spring this year, or doomed to more of what we've suffered through the past fifteen weeks.

Exactly at 11 A.M., Arthur Winthrop, owner of the Pharmacy, will carry outside the "cave" containing the groundhog and, once outside, open its door. The rest will be up to the groundhog. If he comes out and stays out, we can all relax a bit. If he comes out, sees his own shadow, and retreats back into the cave . . . Brr! Time to stock up on more of Winthrop's cold remedies.

EVENT: Prognostication of early or late spring by groundhog.

PLACE: Winthrop's Pharmacy, 154 Main Street

DATE: Monday, February 2nd (Groundhog Day)

TIME: 11 A.M.

CONTACT: Achilles Popeine—(207) 555-1212

And there you have it. The "Who" and the "What" are covered in the line "EVENT" (that is, the "What" is the prognostication of spring, and the "Who" is, of course, the groundhog). The "Where" is obvious, and the "When" is broken up into two lines, date first, time second, just to make it all easier to read at a glance. "Why" is once again implied: because people like to know, even if only in a kidding way, how soon they can expect spring and say goodbye to winter. "Contact" is there just so the editor can easily find your name and number if he has any questions.

This was a rather whimsical release (but not without merit—many's the press agent who's gone out and hired a groundhog in order to grab a little space for a client), so let's close this section with a considerably straighter one. But before we begin, you may be wondering where you should send this kind of release. Almost without exception, it's sent to "News Desk," "Picture Desk," "City Desk," or to the attention of an individual at one of these desks (and in the latter case, it's best to call him about it beforehand, to make sure he'll be there to get the release). Finally, this kind of release demands follow-up. You *must* call to be sure the release has been received. If it hasn't, and there's time, send another one. Sometimes when you reach the desk and you ask if they'll be covering, they'll tell you. More often than not, they'll suggest you check them the day of the event. Do so. That one last nudge often gets you the news coverage that saves your day.

Now here's a more down-to-earth release:

FROM: ERNESTINE STRAIGHT
11 Enterprise Boulevard
Intense, Rhode Island 02889
(401) 555-1212

<u>ATTENTION</u>: CITY DESK

<u>WOMEN'S CLUB TO HAVE MOTHER-DAUGHTER SING
TO LAUNCH "CHARITY WEEK" THIS MONDAY (JULY
12TH) AT GRANGE HALL.</u>

The Intense-Miltown Women's Club will launch its fifth annual "Charity Week" with a Mother-Daughter Sing this Monday (July 12th) at 4 P.M. at Grange Hall.

Three vocal trios, two duos, one quartet, consisting in each case of a mother and her own daughter or daughters, will entertain, as well as the combined forty-voice mother-daughter chorus. Musical selections will include operatic arias, popular songs, folk tunes, and jazz. The show will last till 5 P.M.

EVENT: Mother-Daughter Sing to launch Women's Club's
            "Charity Week."

DATE: Monday, July 12th

TIME: 4 P.M. (till 5 P.M.)

PLACE: Grange Hall, 13 Hicks Street, Intense

CONTACT: Ernestine Straight—(401) 555-1212.

SUMMARY

1. The purpose of a news release, then, is simply that: to impart news. Try to do it in a way that is both interesting and professional-looking. This applies to form as well as content.

Do use a fresh black ribbon in your typewriter. Stay away from colored inks, colored paper, carbon copies.

Always double-space your releases.

Always leave adequate margins around your release.

Type your name, address, and phone number in the upper left-hand corner of the page.

Place your statement of when you want the release to be released slightly lower and to the right. Underline it.

Always use a headline. *Underline* it. Keep it as short as possible.

2. Restate everything in your headline in your first paragraph.

3. Amplify your first paragraph in your succeeding paragraph or paragraphs.

4. Follow up on your releases.

In the case of a release about a news event to a news desk, follow up twice—the first time to see if they've received the release and if there's interest, and the second time on the day of the event to confirm that they're going to cover, or to give them a final nudge if they're still uncertain.

Finally, if the release doesn't make it with the first try, and there's time to try it again, by all means do so, using a different version of the release (even if the facts are necessarily the same). Perseverance, as I keep saying, is the key word in publicity.

7

The Letter

It is my suspicion that the letter has become less and less important as a publicity tool, but it is still fairly significant.

When you're trying to sell a story, your best shot is always to go to the phone. It is more immediate and warmer than the best of letters. It also takes considerably less time. For the most part, these days letters are used as follow-ups, but occasionally a "pitch letter" is still used as the primary lever, usually when the person you're after is housed well beyond the limits of a local call and your client is in no mood to pay for large telephone bills. There are also the scattered few who don't take calls and insist on receiving letters instead.

Let's start with the latter case. You're trying to sell your story cold, via a letter. How do you go about it?

First of all, you try to keep the letter short and to the point. Never underestimate the underlying laziness of all of us. Just looking at the sheer bulk of a long, long letter can make someone weary even before he reads it. Better to read that one later, your outlet may sigh, while hoping that somehow it will disappear in the interim. And sometimes it does.

So keep the letter short and to the point. Also try to make it vital. You're trying to sell something, and the way to sell it is to make it sound interesting, exciting, worthwhile. Your words should indicate this through their own vitality.

A word here about humor: There's no question that humor can

be extremely helpful in making someone receptive to what you're selling, but it can also be a dangerous thing to fool with. Unless I immediately sense a rapport with someone I haven't dealt with before, I never use humor on the telephone. Try to be funny with someone who's on a different humor wavelength, and you can confuse, annoy, or anger him and thereby lose your story. As for people I've dealt with previously on the phone and whom I've gotten to know, it all depends on the person. But a letter is different, I think. If humor seems called for, use it without fear. If the recipient doesn't get the joke the first time, he can reread the puzzling words, and in all likelihood will get them the second time. Intelligent people have a sense of humor, and virtually everyone you'll be dealing with in the press is intelligent. It's just that even intelligent people occasionally go blank at a spoken bon mot, whereas when it's laid before their eyes, they can usually work it out, if they must, on a second or third go-round.

The other letter you'll write is the follow-up letter. You've made your call, given your pitch, and now you're writing to your outlet because he's asked you to. These letters fall into two categories: the letter that re-explains everything, and the letter that simply says, "I'm the guy you talked to, and here's the material you asked for."

There are also two forms of notes that you'll use in the course of doing any extensive amount of publicity. One is much like the last letter mentioned, a casual personal note along with the requested material. The other is the memo you send a client when he's set for an interview, spelling out the time, date, and place.

I think the best way of telling you how to write all of these is simply by showing you, with an explanation every now and then.

Let's assume you still have that PTA bake sale coming up and you're planning to publicize it by getting the local radio show to do an interview with your chairlady, who has a reputation as one of the best bakers in town. It's the kind of show that's interested in such subjects, but the booker at the radio show doesn't take calls, so you've got to try to reach her by letter. Here's what you might say:

123 Graceful Lane
Jacksonville, Alabama 36265
(205) 555-1212

April 1, 1978

Miss Helen Chivers
c/o Mary Shelton Show
WONT
83 Sparks Road
Jacksonville, Alabama 36265

Dear Miss Chivers:

Who makes the best Brown Betty in town? Whose Cherry
Brownies disappear faster than anyone's you've ever known?
Who has simply the best recipe for Key Lime Pie you've ever
tasted?

Your guess might be three different people. My suggestion
is that it is one: Orvaline Wynette, the chairperson of the Jacksonville Elementary School PTA.

The PTA will be holding its annual Bake Sale on May 4th,
and we'd like to publicize it as much as possible. Mrs. Wynette
will be contributing all of her specialties to the sale, and would
be happy to talk about them (and other recipes as well) on your
show. She is a delightfully charming and voluble person, and
I think would provide you with a truly informative and entertaining fifteen minutes.

I'm enclosing some material on the Bake Sale and on Mrs.
Wynette, and, if I may, will call you in a few days on this.

                                        Sincerely,

                                        Wiluda Meyer

You'll note that in the upper right-hand corner Ms. Meyer has
written her address and phone number, and, of course, written her
name at the bottom of the letter. This is to make it easy for Helen
Chivers to either write her or call her.

In the salutation Ms. Meyer has addressed Helen Chivers as

"Miss Chivers." Feminists may get a little annoyed about this, but my feeling is that you shouldn't address anyone as "Ms." unless you know for sure she wants to be called that. You're trying to win people over, not alienate them, and a number of women would be offended at being called "Ms." I've also had assistants in my office wonder whether they should address a woman stranger as "Miss" or "Mrs." These days, with non-marriage no longer being quite the traumatic event (non-event?) it used to be for women, the issue may not be as important, but it seems to me that few women, married or not, object to being called "Miss," whereas a lot of non-married women would object to being called "Mrs."

The opening paragraph is a teaser, the second paragraph an answer to the teaser, and the third paragraph states your business.

The closing paragraph may require a little more explanation. The material you're enclosing should consist of your release on the Bake Sale and, at the very least, one or more of Orvaline Wynette's recipes for the pastries you've described in your opening paragraph. If Mrs. Wynette has ever been interviewed in a newspaper or magazine, you should send a copy of that story along as well (a good Xerox will do, if Mrs. Wynette only has one copy, which she'd like to keep for herself). Finally, why have I had Ms. Meyer say she will call in a few days, when Helen Chivers' policy is not to take calls? Because I've found that often that rule is not hard and fast, and it's always better for the press agent to pursue his outlet whenever possible, rather than passively wait to be called or written to.

Incidentally, if you can't get through when you call and no letter is forthcoming from Miss Chivers after a week or so, send a second letter, with a memo attached that reads something like, "Dear Miss Chivers: Sending this on the chance my first letter went astray." If the letter did go astray, then she's got this one; otherwise, she's had another nudge from you, and this nudge may tip her in your direction. If you receive no reply after this one, then a brief note asking if she's received your letter and if she is interested would be in order. After that? Well, I would hope you would find greener fields to turn to, although I have occasionally pursued the matter even longer. Can't remember whether or not it worked, though.

Here's another letter. The Feature Editor at the local daily is known to be absolutely obsessive about not taking calls—perhaps you found out for yourself when he screamed at you the time you phoned. (This is not something I'm making up—I've run into one like this.) And you do have this terribly important new invention of yours you want to publicize. So once again you turn to a letter.

888 Dearborn Way
Planette, Georgia 30050
(205) 555-1212

December 1, 1982

Mr. Marvin Mehn
Daily Star
Star Plaza
Planette, Georgia 30050

Dear Mr. Mehn:

You can use half the gasoline you're using now, and double the life of your engine. No, I am not trying to sell you something and this is not a crank letter.

I am a graduate of Harvard University, School of Great Inventions, and have been working for the past ten years on a device that would save fuel without damaging the engine in any way or in any other manner impairing the efficiency of an automobile. As the enclosed clippings indicate, I have been successful.

As a resident of Planette, I think my story would be of interest to my fellow citizens, and if you'll study the clippings, I believe you'll agree.

Hoping to hear from you on this, I remain,

Sincerely yours,

Henri Frod

The lead paragraph here is both an eye-opener and a disclaimer. People are quite interested in anything that saves fuel, and since most people drive cars, they're usually personally interested, so it's best to put it on a direct personal basis (*"You can use half the gasoline . . ."*). However, since there have been many claims for this type of invention and none of them seems to have worked, the disclaimer ("No, I'm not trying to sell you something and this is not a crank letter") seems to be called for.

Because there could be a possibility of your being a crank, it's necessary that you state your qualifications, as I have in the second paragraph, and furnish whatever proof you can of those qualifications. The latter would presumably appear in the clippings you've enclosed.

You then state what you're looking for, a feature interview in the *Daily Star,* and close. In this case, if you know for sure your man is an obsessive about the phone, it's wiser not to say a word, but if you don't hear in a week or two, feel free to call before you post another letter. Even obsessives are not always entirely hard and fast about some aspects of their obsessions.

We'll try one more letter of this type, just to clarify the form further. You're doing publicity for a politician who's just starting out, and the nearest big city has a television talk show that would be extremely helpful to him. Again, the talent coordinator insists on receiving pitches exclusively via the mails:

1214 West 42nd St.
Sherman, Mississippi 38869
(202) 555-1212

April 21, 1977

Mr. Archibald Johnson
c/o The Dave Davis Show
KTU-TV
12 Torrance Lane
Montmorency, Mississippi 38945

Dear Mr. Johnson:

Who wants to take the Coca-Cola machines out of the local schools? Who is determined to filibuster day and night against pocket-lining pork-barrel bills in the State Legislature? Who is determined to bring badly needed industry into his county even if it threatens the local ecology?

Lincoln Washington is the man—the most controversial politician to come our way since the late Tarrying John Applegate. Lincoln Washington, a complete unknown two weeks ago, has already begun to quicken the political pulse of this state, as you'll note by the enclosed clippings.

Lincoln Washington is that rare human being, a politician unafraid of taking a stand. You may hate him or you may love him, but one thing is for sure: no one who sees and listens to him is ever indifferent to him. I think he would make a marvelous guest for the Dave Davis Show.

If I may, I'll call you on this in a few days.

Sincerely,

Beauregard Stans

You may wonder, "What if I have no clippings to send? What do I do then?" What you do then is tell the whole story in the letter, or, if you have a press release you can enclose, you tell whatever parts of the story seem to fit best in the letter and let the release furnish the rest of the information. Let's say that you have no clippings on Lincoln Washington; that your letter to the *Dave Davis Show* is your first pitch. Here's how your letter might then read:

1214 West 42nd Street
Sherman, Mississippi 38869
(202) 555-1212

April 21, 1977

Mr. Archibald Johnson
c/o The Dave Davis Show
KTU-TV
12 Torrance Lane
Montmorency, Mississippi 38945

Dear Mr. Johnson:

Who wants to take the Coca-Cola machines out of the local schools? Who is determined to filibuster day and night against pocket-lining pork-barrel bills in the State Legislature? Who is determined to bring badly needed industry into his county even if it threatens the local ecology?

Lincoln Washington is the man—a man who will emerge as the most controversial politician to come our way since the late Tarrying John Applegate. Lincoln Washington is that rare human being, a politician unafraid of taking a stand.

As a used-car salesman, he knows people. His honesty and forthrightness are a local legend in Sherman. His rise from abject poverty to his current position in the community is a story in itself.

There is no question in my mind that Lincoln Washington would make a marvelous guest for the Dave Davis Show. Your audience may love him or your audience may hate him, but one thing is certain: no one who sees or hears Lincoln Washington is ever indifferent to him.

I'm enclosing a press release and, if I may, will call you on this in a few days.

> Sincerely,
>
> Beauregard Stans

And there you have the form. Short, to the point, and as vital as you can make it. Your approach can be softer or harder, straighter or more humorous—that depends on you and your personality. Just keep the basic principles in mind and you'll be all right.

As for the follow-up letter, the letter which accompanies the material you're sending and re-explains what you've already told the person at the other end of the line, the form is not much different. Let's take two previous examples and rewrite them as follow-up letters.

123 Graceful Lane
Jacksonville, Alabama 36265
(205) 555-1212

April 1, 1978

Miss Helen Chivers
c/o Mary Shelton Show
WONT
83 Sparks Road
Jacksonville, Alabama 36265

Dear Miss Chivers:

As I mentioned in our phone conversation today, I think Orvaline Wynette would make an excellent guest for the Mary Shelton Show. There is simply no one who prepares better Brown Betty, Cherry Brownies, or Key Lime Pie, and furthermore, Orvaline has a delightfully charming way of chatting about her baking.

I'm enclosing material on Mrs. Wynette, as well as a release on our annual Bake Sale on May 4th, which is being held at the Jacksonville Elementary School. Orvaline is, of course, the chairperson of the school's PTA, and will be contributing all her baked specialities to the sale.

If I may, I'll call you in a few days on this.

Sincerely,

Wiluda Meyer

And here's our second example:

888 Dearborn Way
Planette, Georgia 30050
(205) 555-1212

December 1, 1982

Mr. Marvin Mehn
Daily Star
Star Plaza
Planette, Georgia 30050

Dear Mr. Mehn:

In accordance with our phone call today, here is some information on myself and my invention.

As a graduate of Harvard University, School of Great Inventions, I have long been involved in a search for a device that would save fuel without damaging the engine or in any other way impairing the efficiency of an automobile. That I have been successful in coming up with an invention that fills these needs, and also cuts fuel consumption in half while doubling the life of the engine, is, I think, proven by the accompanying press clippings.

I believe that, as a resident of Planette, my story would be of interest to your readers, and if you'll study the clippings, I imagine you'll agree.

Hoping to hear from you on this, I remain,

Sincerely yours,

Henri Frod

You won't need more than one example of the follow-up note that's sent along with the requested material, and here's how it goes:

888 Dearborn Way
Planette, Georgia 30050
(205) 555-1212

December 1, 1982

Dear Marvin,

     Here's the material on myself. If I may, I'll call you on this in a few days.

                                       Best,

                                       Henri Frod

Just remember, if you feel you've gotten to know Mr. **Mehn** well enough to address him by his first name, then sign only your first name. (But type your full name below your signature!)

If you've set up an interview for someone, you should always send him a memo, *even though you've already given him the information by telephone.* This is both to ensure against any mistakes being made, and to keep you off the hook should anything go wrong as to time, place, and date. I usually type it on short memo paper so the client can easily carry it with him. Since I have people working for me who may need to refer to a memo if I'm out of the office, I always type in the client's full name. You needn't (unless you're in a similar position) be so formal, but here is the way a memo should basically read:

                          303 West 42nd St.
                          New York, New York 10036
                          (212) 246-1970

                          January 1, 1985

TO: MAX MORATH

     Just to confirm that you're set for the "Today Show" on Wednesday, January 31st, at 5:30 A.M. The address is 30 Rockefeller Plaza, Studio 3G. Our contact is Trinesse Wiener. Remember to bring along your song slides.

                                      Best,

Sometimes you'll want to give the phone number of the interviewer or contact, lest anything go awry, such as the client finding himself late or lost and desperately needing to get in touch with the interviewer. You may also want to let him know how long the interview will last, so he can make other plans, and, as I've indicated above, sometimes you have to remind him to bring along certain materials.

SUMMARY

1. Keep your pitch letter short, to the point, and as vital as possible.

2. Follow-up letters either follow the same form as the pitch letter or are simple "here's the material that you requested" notes.

3. Always send a memo to a client if you've set an interview for him. Mention who the interview's with (both person and outlet, be it newspaper, radio, etc.), where it will take place, and the time. If you're going to be along, say so. Always write both day and date, to avoid uncertainty. If possible, indicate approximately how long the interview should take, and add any special instructions (such as "bring along your record").

8

The Bio

The biography (virtually always referred to as a "bio") is one of the most important tools of the publicist. Like the press release, it tells the story of his client. Often it takes the place of a release. When someone asks for "material" on your client, the bio, if it's up to date, includes everything a release would, and more, so you can send it without any accompanying release. If it needs just a little updating, that can sometimes be done in the note you attach to the bio when you send it out. Similar to the bio is the fact sheet, sometimes known as a "backgrounder." The only difference is that it's not about a person. We'll get to this a little later in the chapter.

I would imagine that everyone has his or her news angle. Since I have handled personal publicity for a number of leading comedians, I thought it might be instructive to show how I handled each of several distinct personalities when it came to writing their bios.

Woody Allen, Joan Rivers, Bill Cosby, Flip Wilson, Rodney Dangerfield, Dick Cavett, David Steinberg, Victor Borge, Robert Klein . . . what was *their* story?

Okay, not Woody Allen, at least not at first. I was so bedazzled by his wit I could think of no way my writing could come close to describing him. So I used other people's bios: the people who wrote about him in the *New York Times,* the *New York Post,* etc. They told the story, and they told it well. Today I do have a bio of Woody Allen, but we'll leave that till later. Meanwhile, let me add that it's often a good idea to enclose good previous news stories on your client when you're sending out his bio. Just be careful not to send your newsman a story by his rival. It might stop you dead.

The fact that someone is funny is not enough when you begin a biography of a comedian. It's what makes him different from all the other funny people—his "newsiness"—that you should try to isolate, and to spotlight at the very beginning of your bio.

With Joan Rivers, the fact that she was a woman separated her from most of the pack. The fact that she could be funny without losing her femininity separated her from all other well-known comediennes when she broke in in 1965. Finally, she was one of those literal "overnight sensations." A wildly successful first *Tonight* appearance that fortuitously was caught by several major TV columnists was the catapult, plus a little adroit cashing in on of same by a quick follow-up barrage of publicity.

I remember Arlene Francis, who has conducted her own New York radio interview show for years, telling Joan that the bio sent her was "the best" she'd ever read. That initial bio seems to be lost to the ages, but the one we did sometime later is, I'm sure, a close approximation.

Watch for what we're doing here. The idea of the bio is to be as full of information as necessary, yet as interesting as you can make it, with the newsiest angle you can find in your lead paragraph. And now, here she is—Joan Rivers!

FROM: RICHARD O'BRIEN
          303 West 42nd St.
          New York, New York 10036
          (212) 246-1970

<u>JOAN RIVERS—HOW TO BE FUNNY</u>
<u>THOUGH FEMININE</u>

Joan Rivers, who became an overnight comedy sensation as

a result of her first "Tonight" appearance with Johnny Carson the evening of February 17, 1965, is that rare comedienne—a girl who is able to be hilariously funny without losing her femininity.

Since then, she has starred repeatedly on the Ed Sullivan and "Tonight" shows, with multiple appearances on TV game shows as well as star stints on the Kraft Music Hall, Dick Cavett show, Mike Douglas show, Merv Griffin show, as guest "Tonight" hostess, and as star of her own morning syndicated TV series.

Joan has virtually taken over New York's famed intimate nightspot, the Downstairs at the Upstairs, has starred at top clubs across the country, including Chicago's Mr. Kelly's, and San Francisco's hungry i, has two comedy albums to her credit, the latest being "The Next-To-Last Joan Rivers Album," on the Buddah label. Joan also makes her singing debut on the new "Vernon Duke Revisited" LP.

Born in Brooklyn and raised in Westchester, Joan began taking acting lessons at the age of 12, and within just a few months was cast for a role in the movie "Mr. Universe," which starred Bert Lahr and a then-unknown actor named Vincent Edwards. ("I've always had a flair for spotting talent," she says. "As soon as I saw him, I predicted he'd never make it.") Her other acting credits are a summer tour to sell-out houses (and critical acclaim) in "Luv" and a brief appearance in the Burt Lancaster movie "The Swimmer" that caused several critics to single her out for her impressive work (among them the reviewers for the New York Times and the Hollywood Reporter).

After graduating from Adelphi Academy, Joan attended Barnard College, majoring in English literature. While in college, she included dramatics in her extra-curricular activities, playing opposite then-unknown actor George Segal.

Upon graduation from Barnard, she went into fashion coordination, and shortly became fashion coordinator for all the Bond stores.

Fashion shows and window designing soon palled, however, and Joan, "having done what you're supposed to do," quit and decided to do what *she* wanted to do, which was to become a comedienne. "I was always fat, right up till I was 14 or 15," she says, "and I was always funny, hoping to win acceptance that way, since I obviously couldn't do it with my looks. And I guess I'm still trying to win acceptance, because though I haven't had a weight problem since my teens, I still *feel* as if I'm fat."

Next came pass-the-hat comedy at the Phase 2 in Greenwich Village, a brief fling with Jack Paar's "Tonight" show, and a part in "Talent 61," a talent showcase which won her a Sunday night audition at Greenwich Village's famed Bon Soir, and a long engagement at the club.

From there, she went to Chicago's Second City, where she stayed for six months. When she returned, she found she'd already been forgotten, and began her "starving period." At scattered intervals came work in the Catskills, replacements for Barbara Harris and Zohra Lampert in New York's "Second City" company, a tour of the Orient with the U.S.O., and a State Department tour of Europe.

She then began writing, creating material for Zsa Zsa Gabor and Phyllis Diller on "Show Street," for Bob Newhart on "The Entertainers," and for Juliet Prowse; she did several of the "Topo the Mouse" sketches for the Ed Sullivan show, and was an idea girl for "Candid Camera."

It was December of 1964 when Joan decided to begin writing for herself and began a long, act-developing engagement at Greenwich Village's Upstairs at the Duplex, which eventually led to her being signed for the "Tonight" show.

Overnight, as a result of "Tonight," her life changed. She

received a recording offer from Warner Bros., nightclub and TV starring offers, and she was lucky enough to have been seen that night by three New York newspaper TV critics, all of whom praised her effusively.

Joan's act is almost completely autobiographical, with very little exaggeration added. "Funny things just happen to me," she explains.

Joan, who married producer Edgar Rosenberg on July 15, 1965, after a whirlwind courtship, has a young daughter, Melissa Frida Rosenberg, born on January 20th, 1968. Friends who remembered her appearing at The Bitter End in Greenwich Village the night she was married weren't too surprised to hear that Melissa, a full-term birth, was born the day after Joan closed a lengthy engagement at Downstairs at the Upstairs, and that two weeks later Joan was discussing the event on the "Tonight" show and preparing to return to the Downstairs in another month.

SIDELIGHTS: Although her success has left her with little spare time, she is an avid reader, as is her husband. When she's not busy writing or performing, Joan reads on the average of a book a day.

She has one sister, a lawyer who was about to get her medical degree also when she met, fell in love with, and married a doctor. The two are look-alikes (the sister is a year older), and during Joan's lean periods the two used to double up on the same temporary jobs, Joan working in the morning and auditioning in the afternoon, and her sister attending medical school in the morning and working in the afternoon.

Once, while "at liberty," she was hired to do promotion for the movie "David and Lisa." She would rush up and down the aisles of art movie theatres screaming "David!" with a young man following her shortly hollering "Lisa!"

Okay, now a few pointers. First of all, you notice we have our same old "FROM," etc., up in the left-hand corner. We also have a headline (often just the name, but in this case it seemed right to include more than just that), but *no* "FOR IMMEDIATE RELEASE, PLEASE." A bio isn't generally meant to be printed (although lazy interviewers sometimes do so), so there's no reason for indicating when you want it published.

Since it's not meant to be printed, the bio is usually single-spaced instead of double-spaced, because there's no need for a newsman to make corrections on it. (The only time I double-space a bio is when there's just not much to say.) A bio is usually just used as a reference, with some segments of it occasionally printed as is (but more often even they are rewritten to some extent).

A bio shouldn't be so long that the interviewer gets tired of reading it, or, even worse, takes a look at it and despairs of reading it. Two pages, I feel, is the absolute maximum, and a page or a page-and-a-half is even better. However, Joan had some anecdotal material which seemed worth using, but as part of the bio would have made it too long. So—and this is one of the few times I've done this—I used the "SIDELIGHTS" format at the end, creating the feeling that the bio had ended, wasn't really long after all, but if you cared to glance at the rest, you might find something of interest. The last two paragraphs, in particular, gave radio or TV interviewers the chance to say, "Tell me about your sister," or "Tell me about the time you were doing promotion for 'David and Lisa,'" and then sit back while Joan went into her story.

Bill Cosby had his own unique angle. Although he was among the first black comedians to emerge, he was not the *first*. But he *was* the first to use material in which race had no bearing. That was news. He was also an ex-football player, certainly an unusual background for a comedian. Somehow his bio has disappeared from my files, but the opening paragraph, at least, would have gone something like this:

Bill Cosby is an original, an ex-football player who's a thinking man's comedian. And a black comedian whose humor is completely without racial overtones.

What set Flip Wilson apart from all the other comics who were coming into prominence in the 1960s was that he was no kid. Furthermore, two other things set him apart. His belief that it takes fifteen full years to flower as a comedian was one. The second was a book he carried everywhere he went, a book in which he jotted down the precepts of comedy, and against which he constantly measured himself. Interesting? Sure. All it took to get these angles was two things: the ability to dig into Flip's past as I interviewed him for the bio, and the ability to spot what gave him newsiness. Two obviously simple things, and they're all you need to get you started on a bio.

Here's Flip:

FROM: RICHARD O'BRIEN
           303 West 42nd St.
           New York, New York 10036
           (212) 246-1970

FLIP WILSON

Flip Wilson is the hottest "new" comic in show business today. He has made scores of appearances on network TV in the past year, starred at top clubs and concerts across the country, and filled the coffers of Atlantic Records with his "Cowboys & Colored People" LP.

Flip may also be the oldest "new" comic in the business. It has taken him fourteen years to hit the top, the first dozen or so of which were spent in almost total obscurity while he went about honing his comedy talents to the degree of perfection he displays today.

The creator of all his own material, Flip was in no hurry to succeed. It is his firm conviction that it takes a comedian 15 years to fully mature, and thus he looked for no success until he'd served his decade and a half of apprenticeship. His devotion to his art is so complete that he has compiled a thick notebook concerning the theory and laws of comedy. After writing a routine, Flip will meticulously check it against his notebook, line for line, word for word. If something deviates from the rules, Flip changes it.

Jersey City-born, Flip made his stage debut at the age of nine in a class play, as Clara Barton, when the feminine lead dropped out and it was discovered Flip was the only one who knew all her lines. At the age of 16, he joined the Air Force, where he got his nickname, "Flip," because of his sense of humor. His commanding officer took an interest in him, and made him take grammar lessons and typing courses, which Flip states enabled him to write all his scripts himself.

Upon his discharge in 1954, Flip was hired as a bellhop by San Francisco's Manor Plaza Hotel. He persuaded the manager to let him do a brief comedy walk-on as a drunk, and his show business career was launched. He hitched across the country from one nightclub to the next, slowly improving the grade of clubs in which he was appearing as time went on and Flip began to find himself.

There is no question he has now not only found himself, but been found. Johnny Carson and Ed Sullivan were his earliest boosters, and he has appeared on their shows repeatedly. Other shows on which he has been a frequent guest of late include the Dean Martin Show, Joey Bishop Show, Rowan & Martin's Laugh-In, Merv Griffin Show, the Mike Douglas Show, and as host on 2 ABC-TV variety shows, "Popendipity" and "Operation Entertainment." Ed Sullivan has signed him for 6 more appearances in 1968. Club appearances include the Frontier Hotel in Las Vegas, the Bitter End, Village Gate and Downstairs at the

Upstairs in New York, the hungry i and Bimbo's in San Francisco, Harrah's in Lake Tahoe, Mr. Kelly's in Chicago, and the Latin Casino in New Jersey.

Also coming up are a second Atlantic LP and, when Flip decides to retire, a book of instruction for young comics, based on the notes Flip has compiled on comedy. They obviously work.

Actually, I could have dug deeper on Flip. I don't remember now whether it was my ineptitude or Flip's unwillingness to disclose the facts, but he had a very difficult early life, so filled with obstacles it's more than a small miracle that he managed to get through alive, much less successfully. It wouldn't, in this case, have been the lead, since his philosophy of comedy was more pertinent, but it could easily have been the third or fourth paragraph, and would have given much more human interest to his story. And of course, for a comic who had nothing else of news value to offer, such a background would have been the lead thought of the bio.

Rodney Dangerfield was a whole other story. Flip was a struggling "new" comic. Rodney had struggled, dropped out—and come back! A few months before Rodney turned up at my office, all over town I'd spotted posters for an art school that were directed at people who were hoping to start their lives all over again, in terms of their careers. And that gave me, when I sat down to write Rodney's bio, my opening paragraph:

FROM: RICHARD O'BRIEN
              303 West 42nd St.
              New York, New York 10036
              (212) 246-1970

RODNEY DANGERFIELD

There was a provocative ad recently for a New York art-school night course that read something like "Gauguin was a bank teller at 35." A night school for comics could go that one even better, using the legend "Rodney Dangerfield was a businessman at 40."

Rodney Dangerfield was born in Babylon, Long Island, on November 22nd, 1921, but it has only been within the past four years that the world has begun to take note of him. It is significant, too, that Rodney sprang, full-bloom, to the attention of the nation's television audiences by making his first TV appearance not with the late-night chatter shows, but on the prime-time apex for comics—the Ed Sullivan Show.

For Dangerfield, all this is actually the second-time-'round with the difference that this time it's working out much more successfully. From age 19 till he was 28, Rodney was a reasonably successful comic on the small-club circuit earning $6,000–$7,000 a year. He was known as Jack Roy in those days, and even then, when it was practically unheard of, always wrote his own material.

But Rodney was married, the future seemed dim, the business difficult, and the constant traveling was a complete drag. For the next dozen years, it was strictly life as a businessman for him.

With just one exception. He couldn't stop thinking funny, and every time he did, he wrote it down. Today he has a duffel bag full of jokes which he dips into whenever he's stuck for a line.

At 40, the comedic juices began stirring more vigorously. Business, it turned out, was even more of a drag. So for a while it was the office on weekdays and the tiny clubs and the mountains on weekends.

Finally he made the decision to go back into comedy on a full-time basis. It was a decision not made lightly, because before things finally began to break for him, Rodney, now a father, had gone $20,000 into debt.

He began writing for other comics, who were impressed with his offbeat, sometimes even off-rhythm approach to comedy lines. But it was when he began playing the Village, at places like the Upstairs at the Duplex, and, later, at 44th Street's Improvisation, that Rodney suddenly became known to Manhattan's talent-bookers.

In October 1965 Rodney was booked into the Living Room. He was highly successful, but the showcase that all comics need—television—wouldn't open up for him. The talk shows, which are the normal first TV steps for a budding comic, remained closed to him. Somehow, the feeling seemed to go, a new 43-year-old comic just couldn't be funny.

Rodney's agents gave up, but not Rodney. "Book me onto Ed Sullivan's dress rehearsal," he said, "that's all I ask." The agents eyed him askance, since the odds against an unknown's being booked as the result of a single performance at the tag end of a rehearsal were astronomical.

But Dangerfield surmounted them. The rehearsal was in October 1966 and Sullivan immediately signed him for his March 5th, 1967, show. A few months later Rodney was at the Copa, and Sullivan caught him. After the show Sullivan rushed up to Dangerfield and told him, "I want to sign you for my show." "You already have," Rodney pointed out, but Sullivan didn't turn a hair, simply signed him for an additional June 4th appearance, with an option for four more, said option not to be picked up until the June 4th appearance.

But Rodney went on March 5th, picked up sensational reviews in "Variety" and "Hollywood Reporter," and his options were happily snapped up, there and then.

Since then, it's been a fast, smooth slide uphill for Rodney. He has made multiple appearances on many of the major TV shows (nearly 40 with Johnny Carson in the past three years) and this year can be seen weekly on NBC's Dean Martin Show, starring as the comedian-owner of a nightclub (a special set was built to resemble his own nitery).

It was on the night of September 29th, 1969, flying in the face of the dire warnings of virtually everyone he knew in the business, that Rodney opened his $250,000 Manhattan nightclub, Dangerfield's. Nightclubs had been in trouble for years, and about the time of Dangerfield's opening went into their worst slump since before the Second World War. Despite this, Dangerfield's has flourished mightily, jamming in crowds with regularity, and playing host to a galaxy of celebrities, among them Milton Berle, Jack Benny, Bob Hope, Johnny Carson, Maureen Stapleton, Buddy Hackett, Shecky Greene, David Frost, Flip Wilson, Joan Rivers, and Totie Fields.

Rodney is also spokesman for the National Conference of Christians and Jews, to whom he has lent his catch phrase, "I Don't Get No Respect." He did a series of "Brotherhood Begins with Respect" TV and radio spots for them (which he paid for out of his own pocket) and recently made some new segments with Jackie Gleason. It is a cause he strongly believes in, with his long-range goal being the introduction of courses in brotherhood into the public schools.

Rodney has also received some glowing notices for his starring role in the movie "The Projectionist" and can be heard on the widely praised LPs "I Don't Get No Respect" (Bell) and "Rodney Dangerfield—The Loser" (Decca).

He is the father of two children, Brian, born October 16th, 1960, and Melanie, born June 12th, 1964.

A few notes here. If your client doesn't object to it, it's a good idea to insert his/her date of birth or current age, since press people often want to know it. Other pertinent dates should be spelled out as well.

Dick Cavett? Unfortunately, I no longer have the bio I wrote before he began his first TV show, an ABC morning program, but here's the one I did before he began his second:

FROM: RICHARD O'BRIEN
         303 West 42nd St.
         New York, New York 10036
         (212) 246-1970

DICK CAVETT

Dick Cavett captured the TV critics of America with his daily morning series on ABC-TV recently, and now ABC is banking on his having the same effect on evening viewers with his new nighttime show (begins May 26th) which can be seen from 10 to 11 P.M. on Mondays, Tuesdays, and Fridays.

Cavett's first work in television was in several dramatic programs. That's when he was an aspiring actor and one of the industry's "most prominent extras," having appeared in the very last "Playhouse 90."

Then he took a job as a copy boy at Time Magazine, where his hours of work allowed him to make the rounds of the casting offices. He was at the same time an avid TV-watcher, particularly of Jack Paar's late-night stanzas. One day Dick read that Paar was constantly worried about his opening monologue. Dick wrote a two-page monologue, went to deliver it, and had the good fortune to bump into Paar himself in a corridor leading to his office. Paar was receptive. Dick wrote a second monologue. Soon he was an ex-copy boy, ex-actor, newly appointed comedy writer on Paar's staff.

When Paar left the "Tonight Show," Dick remained to write for the succession of guest hosts that followed—among them Groucho Marx, Jack E. Leonard, Jack Carter, Soupy Sales, Merv Griffin, Sam Levenson, and Mort Sahl. Later he had comedy-writing assignments with Merv Griffin, for Griffin's day-

time show, the Jerry Lewis show on ABC-TV, and eventually
for Johnny Carson.

About three years ago, Dick decided to write his comedy for
himself and began by appearing at the "in" places like Mr.
Kelly's in Chicago, the hungry i in San Francisco, and the
. Bitter End in New York. As writer-turned-performer, he was
frequently seen on television, where his credits include many
appearances with Carson and Griffin.

In 1967 he starred in "Where It's At," one of the series of
specials on "ABC Stage 67," and in a second special, "What's
In." His ABC morning series began March 4th, 1968.

Cavett, 32, calls Gibbon, Nebraska, his hometown, although
he was actually born in nearby Kearny. Later the Cavetts
moved on to Grand Island, Nebr., and then to Lincoln, where
Dick went to high school with Sandy Dennis. Dick's parents,
Mr. and Mrs. A. B. Cavett, remain residents of Lincoln, where
Dick's dad is a media supervisor at Lincoln High.

A scholarship from Yale brought Dick east to study English
literature. In his senior year he switched over to Yale's drama
school, eventually to do some summer stock in New England.
Dick recalls that at Stratford, Conn., in a production of "The
Merchant of Venice" which starred Katharine Hepburn, he had
his biggest role—one line—and he still remembers: "Gentlemen,
my master Antonio is at his house and desires to speak with
you both."

Eventually Dick came to New York in an attempt to get
bigger lines. As it turned out, he did, and they are a lot funnier.

BIRTHPLACE: Kearny, Nebr. BIRTHDATE: Nov. 19, 1936

Cavett's life was obviously not filled with incident and his approach to comedy not "different," but by this time he had captured the critics of America. That was important—in fact, the
most important thing at that juncture of his career—so I stressed

it in the first paragraph. The Paar anecdote was a good one and was continually used, in interview after interview. You'll notice the birthplace and birthday were handled in a different way in this bio. No particular reason; it just seemed to work out this way. In later bios they were incorporated into the body of the text.

As I say, I don't have the first bio I wrote for Cavett, but I suspect, being able to furnish just a story with only a few human sidelights, I probably spiced it up with some of Dick's more memorable lines. As I did later with another young up-and-coming comedian, David Steinberg:

FROM: RICHARD O'BRIEN
         303 West 42nd St.
         New York, New York 10036
         (212) 246-1970

DAVID STEINBERG

David Steinberg might be described as a wee slip of a lad. He might also be described as: a graduate of Second City; a bright new "Tonight Show" discovery; the proud owner of a controversial new UNI LP, "David Steinberg: The Incredible Shrinking God"; the leading actor in Robert Alan Aurthur's "Carry Me Back to Morningside Heights," with which Sidney Poitier is making his Broadway directorial debut (opening date February 26th, 1968).

An indication of Steinberg's style and trend of humor may be found in the following two incidents:

He was standing outside Chicago's Second City, having his shoes shined, when a hippie wandered by. The hippie glanced at Steinberg, looked away, looked back, then approached him, his Hindu bells tinkling as he moved. "Gee, you look familiar," the hippie said. "Who do you remind me of?"

"God," Steinberg answered. "I remind you of God. That's not surprising. After all, I was made in His image. As a matter of fact, you resemble Him a bit yourself."

The hippie nodded and walked away. . . .

Steinberg made his Broadway debut in Jules Feiffer's "Little Murders." The night of the opening, the producer told the cast, "This play is too serious, too satiric for anything as frivolous as an opening night party. But when the play has run a year, I'll give you a party you'll never forget."

Within a few days after it opened, the producer assembled the cast and told them the play would close that week. There was a silence, and then Steinberg asked, "Does that mean the party is off?"

Steinberg, a 27-year-old Canadian, is the son of a rabbi, and in fact studied to be a rabbi himself. At 15 he left Winnipeg to attend the Yeshiva in Chicago, and at 17 went to Israel, returning at 18 to attend the University of Chicago. He left the University of Chicago in 1962 and the following year joined Chicago's famed Second City company. A few quotes on his work there follow:

"When I first saw David Steinberg it was one of those happy times when you spot someone on a stage and know immediately that a distinctive talent has arrived." (Chicago Daily News)

"David Steinberg is a young man slightly handsomer than Ringo Starr and far cleverer than most humans who ever attempt the elusive art of improvisational theatre." (Cue)

"A natural comic actor, intelligent as well as skillful, Mr. Steinberg not so much practices his trade as embodies it. His timing, speech, facial gestures, all conspire to fix your attention and incite your pleasure; he even moves like a dancer. Best of all is his attitude which I would characterize as benignly nonchalant." (Village Voice)

"David Steinberg is 21 going on 316." (Chicago Sun-Times)

David's credits include the Dean Martin show and two as yet unreleased films: "Frank's Greatest Adventure" and "The Next Place."

He claims his most fervent wish is to play the lead in "The Alan Arkin Story."

Since Steinberg was not well known in New York at this time, yet obviously had made his mark elsewhere, I tried to get this across, through the opening paragraph (impressive credits for an "unknown"), through an indication of his original slant on humor, and through some of his reviews.

Robert Klein was something like Steinberg when I handled his publicity, but more of a problem. He had no "lines," dealing more in descriptive humor, a humor that was more acted out than gagged up. What he gave me of his background was hardly teeming with human interest. But he had compiled an impressive number of credits in an impressive number of areas. So that became my angle, the first two short paragraphs signaling what was to come through the rest of the story:

FROM: RICHARD O'BRIEN
            303 West 42nd St.
            New York, New York 10036
            (212) 246-1970

ROBERT KLEIN

Robert Klein gives every sign of being very much on his way.

At 29, he has made four movies, had his own prime-time network TV show, done four Broadway plays, worked some of the country's top "in" nightclubs, and run up a score or so of appearances on network TV.

Born in the Bronx, he was graduated from DeWitt Clinton High School, received a B.A. from Alfred University, attended the Yale Drama School, and, after working as a substitute teacher in junior high and high schools, made his professional acting debut in 1963 in an off-Broadway production of "Six Characters in Search of an Author."

He later joined Chicago's Second City, and came to Broadway in a Second City production in March of 1966. He then won a role in the Broadway-bound "The Apple Tree." While the show was trying out in Boston, he started to think seriously of becoming a stand-up comedian. He began to write material and practice routines into a tape recorder.

After opening in New York in the show, Klein continued to develop his act, trying it out in small local clubs while still appearing on Broadway. At one of the clubs, The Improvisation, he was seen by comedian Rodney Dangerfield, who recommended him to talent managers Jack Rollins and Charles Joffe, who'd developed the careers of such as Woody Allen and Dick Cavett.

He left "The Apple Tree" and went into nightclubs. Then, in January of 1968 he appeared on network TV for the first time, and a few months later appeared on Broadway in "New Faces." His next Broadway show was "Morning, Noon and Night," in which he received superb notices. At this time he began to turn up regularly on the Johnny Carson, Merv Griffin, Dick Cavett, David Frost, Joey Bishop, Ed Sullivan, and Tom Jones shows. In the past season, in addition to a number of talk show appearances, he has been seen seven times on the Ed Sullivan show, twice on the Flip Wilson show, and once with Tom Jones.

Last summer he became the star of "Comedy Tonight" on CBS-TV, winning high critical praise, and in the past year has co-starred or been featured in the movies "The Landlord," "The Pursuit of Happiness," and "The Owl and the Pussycat," and stars in the forthcoming "The Wound."

Other current projects include a headline engagement at

Greenwich Village's The Bitter End beginning April 28th for one week, and appearances with Dick Cavett on April 23rd, Mike Douglas on April 27th, and Johnny Carson on April 28th. He is also collaborating on a screenplay, has begun a monthly column for the new magazine "You," and has been reading for the Lenny Bruce role in the projected Broadway production.

Highpoints of his career include reading poetry with the Chicago Symphony Orchestra, and playing in a special performance of the musical "Candide" in Corpus Christi, Texas. Less of a highpoint was his first venture into show business—as one of the singing Teen Tones on the Ted Mack Amateur Hour. They lost, Robert claims, "to a one-handed pianist."

But sometimes, when you're dealing with a living legend, all you need are the facts, man. There's no need to sell Victor Borge through a bio; no way, really. He's pre-sold. So in this case, when Victor came to me, all I did was marshal my facts and present them to the world. I have said a bio should run no longer than two pages, and I mean it. But Victor's experience and credits are so vast that I fudged a bit. When I send out his bio, it's on two pages. But they're both legal-size.

FROM: RICHARD O'BRIEN
             303 West 42nd St.
             New York, New York 10036
             (212) 246-1970

VICTOR BORGE

Victor Borge was introduced to the piano at the age of three by his mother. His father, a violinist with the Royal Danish Symphony, later wanted him to study the violin, but Borge was determined to stay with the keyboard, and at the age of 8 made his concert debut in Copenhagen. Overnight he was hailed as a prodigy and won a scholarship to the Copenhagen music conservatory. While still in his teens, Borge studied in Vienna and Berlin, with Frederick Lammond and Egon Petri (one of only four students the famed Petri instructed per year).

Borge had already built a reputation for his concertizing in his tender years, and was augmenting his income as an organist (generally at funerals) when his talent as a humorist was discovered. The local Chamber of Commerce in his native Copenhagen staged an annual revue, one of the major social events of the season, which was performed by amateurs but written by professionals and reviewed by major critics. This event, usually attended by the Royal Family and leading theatrical personalities, was often a springboard for young performers, writers, and composers. When the scheduled headliner of one of these shows fell ill, Borge was asked to replace him, and one of the most significant chapters of his career was written. From that moment he began his dual career as master musician and humorist. Shortly thereafter he became a leading personality and starred on stage and screen.

The word about Borge soon spread beyond the Danish borders, and a tour of Scandinavia followed. It was at this point that Borge completely gave up his straight concertizing. But soon the Nazis' invasion of Denmark temporarily halted his career, as Borge was one of their chief targets. His devastating satire had often been directed at Hitler and all that the swastika stood for. Appearing in Sweden at the time of the fall of Denmark, he caught the last vessel to leave Finland for America. Unable to speak English, and all his Danish belongings impounded, he arrived in the U.S. in 1940 almost penniless.

Although a celebrity in his homeland, Borge was unknown in America, and for the next year he lived on twenty-five cents a day, spending much of his time in movie houses, where he went daily to listen and learn to speak English. Eventually he was heard at a private party, and was asked to do the audience warm-up for a major radio show, succeeding so thoroughly that he was immediately offered a guest appearance on Bing Crosby's Kraft Music Hall radio show.

Hired on a week-to-week basis, Borge remained on the show for fifty-six weeks. Within the second week he was named in a nationwide radio editors' poll as the "comedy find of the year." The "Victor Borge Show," "Lower Basin Street," and other radio hits headed by Borge soon followed. He toured the United States and Canada, from Carnegie Hall to the Hollywood Bowl, and became a leading draw in the fashionable supper clubs and leading hotels in America. Television appearances followed radio, with the extra dimension of sight affording even greater impact to his performances.

In 1953 Borge began to create theatrical history. He had developed a one-man show, and now rented a theatre in Seattle, Washington, for a week's engagement. The house was jammed night after night. An engagement in San Francisco's Curran Theatre and a sweep through Montreal, Detroit, Cincinnati, Philadelphia, Boston, and the Eastern States followed.

But this was all a mere prelude to what New York Times critic Walter Kerr called "The Borge Era of Broadway," which began at the Golden Theatre on October 2nd, 1953.

Experienced theatre people said that a one-man show could never go on Broadway. Borge's made history its first night by paying back its entire investment with that single performance, the only show in history to do so. But that was just the beginning. Three years later, having chalked up a record-shattering 849 performances, Victor Borge's one-man, Tony-nominated show became the longest solo run in the history of the theatre, not only in America, but in the world. He won Broadway's Shubert Award, with the legendary Jake Shubert remarking that it was the first time in his life he had sat through a show from beginning to end.

Since that time his "Comedy in Music" has continued to delight audiences throughout the world, with standing ovations the rule rather than the exception (in England a note on the program at one of his concerts read: "The management is not responsible for articles lost during standing ovations").

He has given command performances for kings and queens and presidents. He has been knighted by the kings of Norway, Denmark, and Sweden and has become known as the Ambassador Plenipotentiary from the United States, twice being honored by the U.S. Congress. His numerous worldwide television appearances include a much-hailed series of specials here.

Marking his thirty-fifth year in the United States as a unique musician and entertainer, Victor Borge is also a much sought-after conductor, and, as such, has added a new dimension to his career. In recent years he has conducted scores of leading symphony orchestras in Europe, Canada, and the United States, including the prestigious Concertgebouw in Amsterdam, the Danish Royal Symphony, and the Philadelphia, Cincinnati, Detroit, and Cleveland Symphonies, to name but a few. For his conducting he has received rave reviews from leading music critics, and twice within three months he completely sold out the Royal Albert Hall in London this year, first with his one-man show, and the second time as conductor and performer with the London Philharmonic Orchestra.

Most recently, while in England, Borge was invited to perform at the Queen's wedding anniversary party, an annual affair given by Lady Zia Wernher, at Luton Hoo Castle. It was an especially memorable evening since, with the event restricted to an intimate family audience, the reaction of the Queen was immediately evident. Her virtually non-stop laughter and her occasional brushing away of the tears of laughter provided an evening that is among Borge's most treasured memories.

Several years ago, when Indiana's Romantic Music Festival was faced with a serious financial crisis, Borge took time out from his heavy touring schedule to conduct the Indianapolis Symphony there, and has been credited with saving the Festival. He is now one of its main pillars, having conducted and otherwise performed there three times to the tumultuous acclaim of both critics and audiences.

This past February, Borge was also credited with saving the winter series of the Oakland Symphony, and in the past has performed similar services for other struggling symphonies, persuading people to subscribe for an entire season in order to see and hear Borge perform.

In another area, he has written, with Robert Sherman, the best-selling "My Favorite Intermissions" (Doubleday), recounting incidents from the lives of the great composers both accurately and hilariously. It is currently in its 7th printing in the U.S., and has been translated into three languages.

What free time Borge has, he spends with his wife, Sanna, their five children, two sons-in-law, and five grandchildren, in the family homes in Greenwich, Connecticut, and St. Croix, Virgin Islands. Or, preferably, sailing together wherever and whenever his schedule and the weather permit, since, as Borge has put it, "With me, the three B's are Bach, Beethoven, and boats."

If Woody Allen is not quite as legendary as Victor Borge, he's on his way. And besides, as I mentioned, I've always been shy of trying to use my own inadequate words to describe Woody Allen. So once again I stuck to the facts:

FROM: RICHARD O'BRIEN
            303 West 42nd St.
            New York, New York 10036
            (212) 246-1970

WOODY ALLEN

Woody Allen has been hailed as one of the most original and multi-faceted wits of our time. The creator of his own material, he performs in nightclubs, TV, on the stage, and in movies.

His first play, "Don't Drink the Water" (1966–68), ran on Broadway 588 performances (and was made into a movie starring Jackie Gleason). His second, "Play It Again, Sam" (1969–70), in which he made his stage debut, was also a hit, chalking up 453 performances, and was also made into a movie (1972), with Woody repeating his Broadway role and doing the screen adaptation.

"What's New, Pussycat?" (1965) was his first movie, both as writer and actor. Next to be released was "What's Up, Tiger Lily?" (1966), for which he concocted the gagged-up, dubbed-in dialogue. "Casino Royale" (1967) was a strictly acting chore, Woody would like everyone to know. With "Take the Money and Run" (1969) he made his directorial debut, as well as co-authoring and starring in the movie. He followed the same three-role path in "Bananas" (1971), "Everything You Always Wanted to Know About Sex (But Were Afraid to Ask)" (1972), and "Sleeper" (1973). His latest, "Love and Death" (1975), found him as full author as well as director and star.

Woody's successful first book, "Getting Even," is available in both hardcover (Random House) and paperback (Paperback Library). His latest, "Without Feathers" (also Random House), has been even more successful, hitting the list of the top ten best-sellers. "Woody Allen, The Nightclub Years 1964–1968," for United Artists, is his most recent album.

A native of Brooklyn, Woody Allen was born on December 1st, 1935. At the age of seventeen, while still attending Midwood High School, he began making money as a gagwriter. He started by sending gags to newspaper columnists. His name began appearing widely, and a press agent hired him to write jokes that could be attributed to his clients.

After graduating from high school, Woody became a writer for a number of top TV shows, including the programs of Sid Caesar, Art Carney, Pat Boone, Carol Channing, and Garry Moore. He also wrote sketches for Broadway revues and material for a number of nightclub comics. He was the recipient of a Sylvania Award for his work on a Sid Caesar special.

In 1961, at the urging of his managers, Jack Rollins and Charles Joffe, Woody began performing his own material at obscure New York niteries, and shortly gave up his $1700-a-week job to toil for $50 a week in small Greenwich Village night spots.

In November of 1962 he began a lengthy, act-polishing engagement at Greenwich Village's The Bitter End, where he was caught by a New York Times reviewer. A highly enthusiastic review followed and Woody was on his way.

Subsequent and frequent appearances on TV gained him further ecstatic notices from the critics as well as nationwide recognition as the freshest and funniest new comedian in years. It was while appearing at the Blue Angel nightclub in New York that Woody was asked to write and star in "What's New, Pussycat?"

Woody Allen lives in Manhattan, does a great deal of writing, and enjoys outdoor sports, as well as jazz clarinet, appearing with his own band, The New Orleans Funeral and Rag Time Orchestra, on Monday nights at Michael's Pub whenever he's in New York. His humorous essays have appeared in the New Yorker, Playboy, Life, New Republic, and Evergreen Review, as well as in several leading newspapers.

I think by now you've probably got the idea, but just so you don't think all bios are written about comedians, here are three bios of "straighter" people. Judy Black was a young model who'd decided to form her own version of Women's Lib, and asked us to help publicize her idea. On her bio, as you'll see, I used a SIDELIGHTS section at the end, since she had so many interesting anecdotes that could be used not only in an interview but in securing an interview. Radio and TV talk shows love anecdotes, so if they know in advance they'll be furnished with them, you're just that much ahead of the game.

FROM: RICHARD O'BRIEN
           303 West 42nd St.
           New York, New York 10036
           (212) 246-1970

JUDY BLACK

No matter what Look Magazine implies, Judy Black doesn't think Women's Lib is crazy. On the other hand, she does think it has some real problems, and she intends to do something about it.

Judy, the "She Thinks Women's Lib Is Crazy. Why?" cover girl on the March 9th, 1971, issue of Look, is vehemently opposed to such supine anti-Libbers as The Pussycats and "Fascinating Womanhood," but feels that Women's Lib as it stands today is doomed unless it enlists men as supporters and enhances rather than worsens male-female relationships.

To this end, Judy has created a new symbol of women's liberation, derived from the clenched-hand-female symbol now employed by Women's Lib. Judy's symbol consists of the female symbol turning into a soaring dove.

In one instance, however, she may go further than most militant Women's Libbers. She objects strongly to the fact that a woman loses her identity—her last name—when she marries, and that only the man's name can be passed down through the generations. This is male supremacy at its most naked, and she has her own simple solution for it.

Judy Black provides some unexpected depth to go along with and back up her ideas. Although she is probably Washington, D.C.'s top-paid model, she is far from the mindless creature that many people associate with that profession.

A graduate of Briarcliff College, Judy was a childhood rebel who at fifteen found many of the answers she was seeking in Emerson and Ibsen. Scouted by the Captain of the Equestrian Team to compete in the Olympics, she immediately stopped riding, deciding the "minks and manure" life was not for her.

While at Briarcliff she founded a successful program in Ossining, New York, to give culturally deprived black children a direction for their energies.

She left after her first year to join the Peace Corps. Because of the results of a terrible car accident a few years before (she had 108 stitches in her face and head, and had all but one eye covered by bandages for three months), she was rejected on physical grounds, returned to Briarcliff, finished out her final year, and then flew to Paris, ostensibly to study at the Sorbonne.

In fact, once in Paris, she left for Africa, hitched through the Sahara on the back of a lemon truck, and eventually landed in Guinea, where she married her childhood sweetheart in both native and church ceremonies. He was a member of the Peace Corps, and the two of them somehow managed to live (and just barely) on his salary (she *lost* eight pounds during her pregnancy, and, of the four white women there who were pregnant, was the only one not to lose her child).

While in Guinea, Judy taught art to children and became involved with the Food For Peace program.

Returning to the United States, she began modeling in Washington, having previously modeled while at Briarcliff. When she began, Washington had no model's rate, and many models were paid just $5.00 a job. She established one for herself—$35 an hour—and didn't work. But nearby Baltimore proved a little more modern in its thinking, and as Judy's work seeped back to Washington, she began getting calls—and her rate is now $50 an hour.

Judy Black's attitude toward Women's Liberation is summed up thusly: "If there is to be true freedom and an end to war and poverty and human indignities, we as men and women must first get together to create new attitudes which are commensurate with this new age we live in."

SIDELIGHTS: After her accident, Judy's parents promised her she could have "anything she wanted." Out of the blue, she decided she wanted to climb mountains. Her parents gulped, but didn't renege, and as soon as she could, with her head still partially bandaged, Judy flew West, to climb. Her first attempt was Mt. Rainier—quite a task after having been hospitalized for three months. At one point she had to lift each leg with her hands to enable herself to move forward . . . but on the third day she reached the top.

The most terrifying experience of her life came on another climbing expedition, when she fell, knowing in advance that she was going to fall, and dangled hundreds of feet in the air, held only by a rope.

When married in Guinea in the native ceremony, she had to swear that she was at least twelve-and-a-half years of age and promise to give all her cattle to her husband.

While trying to get the Food For Peace program started, Judy and her then-husband traveled throughout Guinea, most of which has no real roads. They had eighteen flat tires on one trip and their native driver finally had to strip the rubber off the rubber trees and tie it to their tires to keep them going. Judy also, out of necessity, learned to fix engines with hairpins.

Once, in Guinea, Judy was brought to an old woman who'd never seen a white woman before. The old woman took Judy's hand and began scratching it, to see if the white came off.

While hitching through the Sahara in the lemon truck, suddenly, in the middle of nowhere, a Citroën drew up, and its driver frantically signaled the truck to halt. When it did so, the Citroën owner got out, walked to the back of the truck, where Judy was riding, said "Auf Wiedersehen," and left.

At 16, Judy went to London with her mother, decided she wanted to act, auditioned for the Guildhall of Music and Drama there, and was accepted. Her mother persuaded her to return home, telling her if she did, she'd let her go to a local high school rather than return to a girls' academy which she hated. So Judy returned, but for a year took a drama course in Villanova, it never being found out that she was a high school student, and even performed in one production.

After her near-fatal accident, with her face encased in bandages, although she worried about what she would look like, Judy felt, she says, an enormous relief that she would no longer be considered beautiful.

Tim Holland, the world's backgammon champ, had everything going for him, so we played it that way.

FROM: RICHARD O'BRIEN
        303 West 42nd St.
        New York, New York 10036
        (212) 246-1970

<u>TIM HOLLAND</u>

Tim Holland, no question about it, is the world's leading player of backgammon. It's a skill that last year won him some $60,000 in prize money and the International Backgammon Championship for the third time. He has also won the World's Championship of backgammon for three consecutive years.

Tim, who in a Harper's Bazaar magazine poll was judged to be the best player by his peers, was already a tournament golf player and an expert in bridge and gin rummy when he happened upon backgammon in 1958. He has since gone on to win more major tournaments than anyone else. He plays aggressively and imaginatively, challenging famous stars, sports figures, royalty, businessmen, and backgammon experts, traveling around the world to do so.

Now that he's had his share of winning, Tim wants to introduce this aristocratic pastime to the common folk, to spread the fun around. To this end, he wrote the best-selling "Beginning Backgammon" (McKay), developed a self-teaching game, "Autobackgammon," designed backgammon boards (Reiss Games), and travels around the country running backgammon tournaments and giving lessons and lectures.

His new book, "Better Backgammon," will be published by David McKay this fall, and he's currently working on a third for them, "The Best of Backgammon."

"Backgammon's finally catching on in this country," he says, "because it's fast, simple, and glamorous."

Probably the oldest game in recorded history, dating back some 4500 years in the Mideast, backgammon was played by Greek and Roman nobility, who passed it on to the English, where it remained a game of the upper classes. In the days of Richard the Lionhearted, gaining permission to play backgammon was one of the benefits of being a knight.

Articulate and an effective teacher of backgammon (he has been paid $3000 for four hours of instruction), Tim is, at age 43, tall (6'3"), darkly handsome, debonair, and charming. Currently married (for the third time) to lovely red-haired Lona Holland, Tim has a 13-year-old son who lives with his ex-wife, now Mrs. Johnny Carson.

He is an excellent golfer and athlete. He won the Long Island Amateur Golf Championship three times in a row, was the Cuban National Amateur Champion the year before Castro came into power, and was a finalist in the French National Championship and a semi-finalist in the British Amateur.

Although being an athlete has helped him in backgammon, Tim is happy his golf days are behind him. His good friend, actor Sean Connery, who used to meet him at the London airport with golf clubs in hand, even in the rain, now meets him with a backgammon set, and to Tim, who likes his creature comforts, that's a happier experience.

Finally, Nicholas is a New York make-up artist and hairdresser who came to us for a few weeks of publicity. His bio was necessarily geared to giving the facts that would attract the editor of a beauty page. The prices at the end of the bio are furnished, since in this case they are as essential as a birth date would be in another bio.

FROM: RICHARD O'BRIEN
        303 West 42nd St.
        New York, New York 10036
        (212) 246-1970

NICHOLAS

Charming, bright, with riveting good looks, make-up artist and hairdresser Nicholas has just returned to New York after an extensive cross-country tour with famed make-up artist George Masters.

Nicholas, a protégé of Masters, studied hairdressing in Paris with Antoine and hair coloring there in the L'Oréal school.

Returning to the States, he worked at Saks in Beverly Hills and then moved to Saks Fifth Avenue in New York, after coming for a visit and deciding to stay.

Nicholas now operates his own salon at 925 Lexington Avenue (68th Street).

His client list includes Evelyn Lauder (of Estee Lauder), who has been a client for over 10 years, Mrs. Clark Gable, Lee Remick, Mrs. Jack Benny, and Vivian Blaine, and many TV commercial actress-models, including Lovelady Powell, Joan Anderson, and Ann Williams, to name a few.

Nicholas is frequently called upon to do TV commercials and magazine ads for Clairol, Revlon, Breck, and L'Oréal.

PRICES AT NICHOLAS SALON ARE:

Make-up and Hair $50

2 Hour Make-up Lesson
(Nicholas does half the face and client does other half)
.... $100

First Hair Cut $25

Set $10

Coloring $25
and up

Now, here's an example of a good fact sheet, an invention that my client Victor Borge was interested in at one time. When we received this fact sheet, it came in a Press Kit that included a letter, a release, a biography, and three pictures. A very well-done package, and, as you'll see, the fact sheet is broken down into separate parts, to make it seem like easier reading.

TYMPONIC CORPORATION

Box 1415   Contact: Michael Isser
Bayville, New York, 11709   (516) 628-1906

FACT SHEET

COTTELL ULTRASONIC REACTOR

Its Significance

Its unique ability to concentrate an enormous disruptive force
into a continuously moving stream enables the Cottell Ultrasonic Reactor to produce a water-in-oil emulsion that gets more
energy out of the fuel, while reducing pollution by the same
percentage of water used. It also effects a reduction in the
pollutants generated by combustion.

The reactor produces boiler operating efficiencies close to 100
percent in home heating applications, and can also be applied
to all forms of oil in automobiles, ships, and airplanes. The
result could be a 33 percent increase in oil resources and a
marked decrease in air pollution.

The reactor is also a breakthrough in the processing tech-
nology whereby the process carried any number of liquids
through an intensive ultrasonic field to produce super-mixed
liquid-liquid or liquid-solid systems. This energy emulsifies oil
and water without the aid of an emulsifier, breaks down cells,
ruptures crystals and disperses agglomerates.

How It Works

The reactor's generator operates on normal 60-cycle electricity
and transforms it into 20,000 cycles per second of alternating
current, created through vibrating crystals. The water-oil mixture in the reactor cannot vibrate that fast, and tiny particles
of oil and water are ruptured (cavitation).

The process provides such force and intensity (over one mil-
lion psi) that the surface area of the water is increased millions

of times. The two liquids form a white emulsion in which tiny particles of water are dispersed in the oil, and the resulting mixture is a fuel that is more lubricating than gasoline. The heat taken up by the water also inhibits the formation of photo-chemical oxides and other pollutants.

Its History

The Ultrasonic Reactor has undergone 3½ years of research and exhaustive testing. Hundreds of measurements have been taken, and inventor Eric Cottell says it took him "3½ minutes to think up and 3½ years to create."

Tests recently conducted by Dr. Vito Agosta, Dr. Sanford Hammer and Professor Clifford Wojan—three of the country's top authorities on combustion and rocketry—confirmed Cottell's findings that the process is yielding significant increases in energy.

How It's Used

Inventor Cottell has licensed the application of his invention for oil heating systems to the Tymponic Corporation in Bayville, New York, which is presently preparing to commercially exploit the product in this industry.

The reactor, installed between the oil burner and fuel tank—and hooked up to a water supply—is ready now to go into commercial applications in large installations such as apartment and office buildings. The unit would be designed and sized specifically for each installation, probably ranging between 5 and 15 horsepower in size for the average apartment and office building. It would be installed and serviced by the Tymponic Corporation.

Finally, whenever I'm dealing with a large number of people (anyone handling a theater company or an orchestra would find this helpful), I use a bio form (see pages 118–19), which I

FROM: RICHARD O'BRIEN   ***PLEASE FILL OUT THIS FORM AS COMPLETELY AS

       303 West 42nd St.   POSSIBLE FOR THE PUBLICITY DEPARTMENT OF THE

       New York, N.Y. 10036   SHOW AND RETURN TO STAGE MANAGER WITH PICTURES,

       (212) 246-1970   IF POSSIBLE.

NAME:_____   TELEPHONE:_____

ADDRESS:_____   DATE OF BIRTH:_____

EDUCATION:_____   PLACE OF BIRTH:_____

AGENT OR MANAGER (NAME & PHONE)_____

IF MARRIED, GIVE SPOUSE'S NAME AND OCCUPATION:_____

_____

CHILDREN AND AGES:_____

ROLE IN PLAY:_____

_____

HOW DID YOU GET YOUR PRESENT ROLE?_____

_____

_____

LIST YOUR PAST SHOWS CHRONOLOGICALLY - UNDERLINE MAJOR SHOWS:

(except Films, Radio, TV)

WHAT   WHERE   WHEN

_____   _____   _____

_____   _____   _____

_____   _____   _____

_____   _____   _____

_____   _____   _____

_____   _____   _____

_____   _____   _____

LIST ANY RADIO, TV, FILM, OR NIGHTCLUB EXPERIENCE:

_____   _____   _____

_____   _____   _____

_____   _____   _____

_____   _____   _____

_____   _____   _____

OTHER BACKGROUND EXPERIENCES, INCLUDING WHERE, WHEN, WHAT YOUR FIRST STAGE
EXPERIENCE WAS:_____
_____
_____
_____
_____
_____

LIST JOBS OUTSIDE THE THEATRE:_____
_____

LIST SCHOOLS YOU'VE ATTENDED:_____
_____
_____
_____
_____
_____

WHAT PHOTOGRAPHER HAS PICTURES OF YOU?_____
_____

ANY MEMBERS OF YOUR FAMILY IN THE THEATRE?_____
_____

ANY MEMBERS OF YOUR FAMILY IN THE NEWS OR WORTHY OF PUBLICITY ATTENTION?_____

INCIDENTS OF YOUR LIFE THAT COULD BE HELPFUL TO PUBLICITY DEPARTMENT (ANECDOTES,
ETC.):_____
_____
_____

HOBBIES:_____
_____
_____

CAN YOU THINK OF ANYTHING ELSE THAT MAY BE HELPFUL TO THE PUBLICITY DEPARTMENT
IN PUBLICIZING YOU? _____
_____
_____
_____
_____
_____

ask them to fill out. It's not nearly as good as a personal interview, but when you don't have time to interview everyone concerned, it can prove helpful.

SUMMARY

1. A good bio or fact sheet should make interesting reading. It should be filled with all of the essential facts relating to the subject you're writing about. In addition, the more human interest the better. It often becomes the central theme of the interview, and without it you might never get the interview.

2. Remember to have your name, address, and phone number in the upper-left-hand corner of the page, or, if that would make you run onto a second page, just run the whole thing across the top of the page like this:

FROM: RICHARD O'BRIEN 303 West 42nd St. (212)246-1970

3. Remember to single-space.

4. Try for a lead paragraph that catches the eye as well as the essence of what you're trying to promote. Try to close with a paragraph that gives the flavor of the individual in an interesting, even entertaining way.

9

The Telephone: How to Use It

I sometimes find it amusing when I remember that as a child I was terrified of the telephone. When everyone else was out of the house and I was expected to answer the phone, I'd pray that it wouldn't ring. If anyone had told me at the age of seven, say, that my life's work would consist in large part of making telephone call after telephone call, I'd have thrown myself off the nearest stoop.

Even up to a few years ago, if a call had to be made at home and I had a choice, I'd wistfully ask my wife to do it.

But in the office, making phone calls is no harder for me than anything else I have to do (it's all hard, of course—I have to kick myself every morning to get myself started, and I need plenty of self-nudges along the way the rest of the day). And it's certainly one of the most satisfying aspects of publicity, because it can be the easiest way of getting publicity for your client.

You pick up the phone, dial it, get your party, tell him your story, and he tells you "okay." What could be easier?

Of course, it doesn't always work out that way. Sometimes the call is a preliminary to a letter or a release. Sometimes it's a follow-up on a call you've made before (or thirty calls you've made before). Sometimes you're even told "No." But, ah, those "Okay" times!

As in anything else, there are right ways and wrong ways to use a phone. Being so unfamiliar with the story you're trying to sell that you stutter and stammer and take terribly long pauses can do you in, no matter how sensational your cause. (A *little* stuttering and stammering is okay. I sometimes have the feeling—and I do it at times, though not intentionally—that it can even be better than being too much in command. This way the contact at the other end of the phone is more likely to be sympathetic than rivalrous, and therefore more inclined to give you a break. But don't *try* to cultivate a little stammering—just relax when it happens.)

Being too aggressive can be a handicap, as can be being too soft a salesman. Calling too many times when you're following up on something one of your outlets is considering can not only lose you that opportunity, but may keep you from ever being able to talk to him or her about any other project you're working on. Some professional press agents are so abrasive that many press people just won't take their calls under any circumstances.

But I think the greatest sin of all in working with the phone when you're doing publicity is not *listening*. Sure, you're there to sell, but you have to be at all times aware of *whom* you're selling to, and when I say that, I mean not only who he is, but who he is at the *moment*.

Even the most easy-going of talent-coordinators can sometimes be hard-pressed and in a hurry to get something done. His voice will usually indicate this, and if, after hearing that tone, you persist in discussing the weather, his children, your children, before getting to the business at hand, you're setting yourself up for a rejection.

Sometimes you call a press person at home, and if you're not listening carefully, you won't realize that he's still half asleep and that he may not remember a word of your conversation once you've hung up the phone. If he sounds groggy, ask if perhaps you've called too early and if he'd like you to call back later. And sometimes it is obvious from the person's tone of voice that he has no time to listen to you at all. If you sense this, say "You sound busy," and if he says "Yes, I am," ask if he'd rather you call back later. And if it sounds as if he can take one more question, ask what the best time would be.

This doesn't cover it all, of course. There are all sorts of nuances to listen for. You can sometimes tell, for instance, when interest is flagging, or when the person is ready to be sold. *Listen.* You'll hear it.

The first step in any press campaign is getting your facts down on paper—a press release and, usually, a bio. The next step can be either mailing out your releases or making phone calls. It depends on the situation.

Generally, when I begin a campaign, I like to get things moving fast. So, once my initial release and bio are written and printed, I try to get the release out and some calls made on the same day. If I can set up a few interviews, it gives me a boost, the client a boost, and of course gets the news out that much faster.

The things you use the phone for in publicity are basically to make an initial contact (that is, to find out to whom you should send your release or letter); to make a pitch (a "pitch" means trying to sell your client, generally for a press or radio or TV interview); and to follow up on releases, on letters, and on the mailing of requested material you have sent to the outlet.

If you're making an initial call (or, more likely, a set of calls), a good idea is to read through your release first, familiarizing yourself with it. Keep it in front of you. If, while on the phone, you find yourself bogging down on the facts, you can run your eyes over the release and extemporize details, or even read them straight from the release as long as you don't let it sound as if you're reading. Your conversations on the phone should always sound spontaneous. You're selling news. You're going to sound much more immediate, and therefore newsier, if what you say sounds spontaneous, rather than having the ring of something already said (written) in the past.

An initial call goes something like this, once you've got the party you're after:

"Hello, this is Arthur A. Chester. I'm handling publicity for a new book about self-surgery, called *The Kindest Cut*. It's written by the world's most famous self-surgeon, Dwight Turner. It's just been published by Barter & Lee, and I just wondered if you might be interested in doing an interview with him." (Or "having him on your show," if you're talking to a radio or TV booker.)

At this point, the person on the other end of the phone says, if you're lucky, "Oh, yeah, sounds interesting. When is he available?"

This can be an embarrassing moment if you don't know. So before you make any calls, be sure that you know exactly when your client is available. Have his schedule written down, and close at hand.

If the response is just that simple—"Sounds interesting—when is he available?"—you just tell them when, and if you're lucky again, the person you're calling will say, "Okay. Make it this Tuesday at two o'clock."

"Fine. Tuesday at two o'clock. You mean P.M., I guess?" Because usually they do, but sometimes they don't, and having a client turn up for an interview twelve hours before or after the time can be pretty embarrassing for you. So do be careful of this.

Next, you either ask where he's to go or, if you already know, repeat the address, just to make sure it's still the same (people do move, and they often don't tell you), and find out whom the client is to ask for. Next, call the client to confirm it with him. (*Never* assume it's okay without checking first.) Then send him a memo with all the facts.

Sometimes, if it's a newspaper or magazine interview, you or the reporter will suggest that the interview be conducted at a restaurant over lunch or drinks. If so, then it's up to you, once the interview is set, to get back on the phone and make a reservation. (Generally, when it's done by professionals, a reservation for three people—the press agent usually goes along with the news-paperman and the client. However, for most of those who read this book, it will probably be just for two—the client, who could easily be yourself, and the newsman.) Make the reservation in the name of the person being interviewed. And tell the newsman, while you're still on the phone, that the reservation will be in the client's name. Otherwise, he may turn up at the restaurant, ask for a table reserved in your or his name, find there's none, and either leave or sit at the wrong table and miss you. Believe me, it's happened. More than once.

However, not infrequently, after you give your client's schedule, the person you're speaking to says, "Okay, let me check and I'll call you back."

Well, he often doesn't. Sometimes he specifies when he'll call back ("I'll call you before the end of the day"), and then your course is clear. If he hasn't called by the self-imposed deadline, it's all right to then call him and say something like, "Hi, this is Arthur A. Chester. Just wondered if you knew yet when you might be able to see Dwight Turner, the self-surgeon."

If he doesn't pick a time when he's going to call you back, then you'll have to decide when to call him. Most of the time, the next day is okay. *But make sure,* if he doesn't call you, *that you call him.* Too many interviews are lost simply because press agents don't follow up.

More often, when you call about an interview (particularly if you're not someone well known to the contact), you're asked to send material before he'll make a decision. This can consist of a letter, a release, and a bio, or maybe just a letter and a release or a letter and a bio, or sometimes a brief note along with release and/or bio. If it's just a note you're sending with the material, it can read as casually as:

Dear Jim,

Here's the material on self-surgeon Dwight Turner and "The Kindest Cut." If I may, I'll call you on this in a few days.

Sincerely,

And even if you mayn't, you call him anyway.

At other times you may be told, "Gee, I haven't heard of the book. Can you tell me something about it?"

And once more you find that it's helpful to be more than conversant with your subject, and also helpful to have a release at hand to glance at or read from, should you suddenly go blank somewhere along the way. After all this, he may be sold, or he may say something like, "I don't know. We've had an awful lot about medicine lately."

Now's the time to pull out all the stops. Whatever cards you've got to play, use them, even if you have to repeat yourself. (It's better not to repeat, if you can avoid it, since you didn't sell him with it the first time. But if that's all you've got, then use it—you may do a better job the second time around.) You might come up with something like, "Yes, but this is different. Self-surgery has suddenly become as big as tennis in certain circles. And Turner knows the subject backward and forward. He can really talk about it. . . . He's an extremely verbal man, as a matter of fact, very intelligent, informed, and to the point."

Whatever you come up with, the point is to not give up until you're given a flat "no." Until that moment, there is always hope. People are persuadable. Certainly there are times when you'll run across someone who just isn't interested in self-surgery and never will be. Sometimes you're just calling the wrong person—it's not the kind of subject he'd ever touch. And sometimes too much has been said about the subject already. But generally, if what you're pitching has any value at all, the person at the other end of the line can be persuaded. (Sometimes, I will admit, not by you. It's amazing the different things two press agents can come up with—and strike out with—on the same project. You can't expect to win all the time, but if you at least give it your best shot, you can't have any regrets.)

Just a word here about what you do when you're asked to send out material. *Send it out the same day*. People appreciate, and are impressed by, efficiency. The message implicit with your package is that it is important to you and therefore it should be important to them. If you wait a couple of days to get around to mailing it, the person you're sending it to may have cooled off, maybe even forgotten your call, and in any case not be very impressed by your slowness in following through. Lastly, the more quickly you send it out, the more quickly you can follow up, and time is generally of the essence in publicity.

Oh, and if you're given a flat "no," you still have one last card, "Well, is there anyone else at the station (paper, magazine) who might be interested in this?" Often there is, but if you don't ask, the newsman generally won't think of it. And rejection is no fun, but if he leads you on to someone else who says "yes," you won't feel you were rejected by him at all—just referred.

What about the approach on the phone? Hard-sell? Soft-sell? I said before that too hard a sell is wrong, and too soft a sell is wrong, but the stress should be on the word *too*. Both hard-sell and soft-sell can be effective. It just depends on who's using them. The important thing is to be true to yourself. If you're not a hard-sell person, don't try it. And vice versa.

These days the soft-sell seems to be much in vogue, after the years of hard-sell that lasted into the early 1960s. I've been told I'm soft-sell, but I don't think of it that way.

My approach has always been to talk to someone in the press as if he's at least as intelligent as I (no doubt with excellent reason), and to treat him the way I'd want to be treated if the situation were reversed. I'd want to be treated as if people felt I had the intelligence and background to decide things for myself, that I needed to have nothing underlined or spelled out as if I were a child. I'd expect to be told the truth.

A press agent has to believe in what he's selling. But that doesn't mean he has to believe in it *fully*—in its every ramification. More times than I care to think about, when I've been hired to handle other press agents' clients (usually a California press agent who needs representation in New York for a client), I've found people on my hands whose talent was (at least in my mind) highly questionable. But I might think that the client's story or an aspect of his or her personality was newsworthy and merited attention. And my approach would not be to say "I've got this great new singer who's going to be the next Barbra Streisand," but simply "I've got this new singer who was born in a log cabin on Staten Island and raised twelve brothers and sisters herself from the age of three."

What I'm saying is, find what interests you about the client, what you personally think is important. Sometimes it can even be "Everyone is talking about her. She's had superb reviews wherever she's played." No need to mention that you personally think the reviewers are wrong. After all, it's just as likely that *you* are. Seize on what is important (and truthful) to you, and what you think will be important to the person you're going after. Then sell it.

If you are a hard-sell type, don't fight it. Sure, you may turn off some people, but others will be charmed by your courage and forthrightness. I remember one columnist smilingly remembering a high-powered self-promoter "whose eyeballs were almost bursting out of his head" with eagerness. The columnist found him so refreshing and amusing that he devoted a whole column to the man's enterprise.

Just remember, hard-sell doesn't mean hostile or abrasive. That can lose you too much. And soft-sell doesn't mean being so hesitant and without confidence that you can't hold people's interest. You've got a story to tell. Tell it the best way you know how. When you're on the phone, make yourself sound enthusiastic, confident, even excited if the event or client merits it. Be "up," even if you're soft-sell. It's not a question of lying to yourself. If you don't feel "up," just change your mood. You can do it.

SUMMARY

1. Know your facts before you call. (Keep them handy, should you suddenly go blank.)

2. Keep your client's schedule of availability at hand.

3. If you're asked to send out material, send it out the same day.

4. If you've set up an interview for a client, confirm it with him, and send him a memo about it, *the same day*.

5. If you have to make reservations, either make them that day or, if you work with a desk calendar, jot it down for the day you think you should make the call.

6. *Listen* as well as talk. Listen for the mood of the person you're speaking to, both at the beginning of the call and through all its fluctuations.

7. Believe in what you're trying to sell. If you can't believe in it totally, try to find some aspects that you do believe in, and use only those in your approach. If you don't believe in any of it, then you shouldn't do it at all. Even if you score an occasional success, the way you feel about yourself at the end of it all won't be worth it.

8. Hard-sell or soft-sell, use whatever approach you're most comfortable with.

9. Treat the man or woman at the other end of the phone the way you would yourself. Respect his intelligence.

10

The Column Item

My favorite part of doing publicity is the column item. You sit, you think, you type, and you mail it out. And a few days later, if you're lucky, there it is, staring back at you from the pages of a newspaper.

Perhaps I'd better explain first what a column item is. In years of dealing with entertainers who were going to appear at the clubs I was handling, I would ask them for pictures, bios, and any kind of news or anecdote that I could use for a column item. "What do you mean, column item?" has been the usual response.

A column item is a bit of news, an anecdote, a joke, that can be used in a column by a columnist. Most newspapers have columnists. Earl Wilson and Jack O'Brian are two of the country's leading syndicated columnists. Their columns are devoted, for the most part, to the doings of people in the entertainment world. Much of the news they dig up themselves. But there is plenty of other news out there that they won't necessarily happen upon, so when they get an interesting, newsy item from a press agent, they use it. The same for a good anecdote or joke.

At one time the columnist was an enormous force in the entertainment world. A press agent could make a fine living by being "tight" with only Walter Winchell, for instance, When I began in the business, in 1960, the columns were beginning their decline, but even then the right kind of three-or-four-line item about a restaurant in Dorothy Kilgallen's column could ensure that restaurant being packed to the rafters for at least two weeks after the item had run.

Today this is no longer true. Columnists don't have the power they once had. In fact, up until not too long ago, columns seemed to be on their way out. If a columnist quit, died, was fired, no other columnist replaced him. But in the past few years there has been a small resurgence of the old-style personal columnist, and, more significantly, a number of columns where the readers write in, asking questions.

These question columns are not all they seem. Often the questions are asked by the columnists themselves, since they know the answers. Sometimes they are asked by press agents, who not only ask a question about one of their own clients, but furnish the answer. At other times the columnist even calls the press agent and asks him to come up with a question-and-answer. So many, if not all, of these columns can be approached by anyone with something of note to contribute, even if it's something that's going to blow his own (or his client's) horn.

Naturally, Earl Wilson or Jack O'Brian is not going to run an item about a Ladies' Auxiliary's Las Vegas Nite (unless, of course, Elizabeth Taylor is somehow a member of that Ladies' Auxiliary). But a columnist on a local paper may find the item worth using.

Let's take a few examples and show just how you can go about figuring out how to write a column item on something you're publicizing.

Let's start with that PTA bake sale. Here are some sample straight news items that you might send to a local columnist:

> The annual PTA Bake Sale will be held at Jacksonville Elementary School on Monday (May 4th), in the gymnasium.

*

> The annual PTA Bake Sale will be held at Jacksonville Elementary School on May 4th from 9 A.M. to 4 P.M.

Proceeds from the annual PTA Bake Sale, being held May 4th in the Jacksonville Elementary School gymnasium, will be used to buy new books and supplies for the school's library.

*

Orvaline Wynette, Wiluda Meyer, and Jane Smith are in charge of the annual PTA Bake Sale, taking place at Jacksonville Elementary School, in the gymnasium, on May 4th.

*

Orvaline Wynette, Wiluda Meyer, and Jane Smith, heading the May 4th PTA Bake Sale at the Jacksonville Elementary School, would like to hear from anyone who'd like to contribute cakes, pies, or cookies to the event. They can be reached through the school's office.

Of the five straight-news column items above, at least four could be sent, at varying times, to the same columnist, since each contains different items of information. More likely, if there was more than one columnist around who'd be interested in these items, you'd send one to one, another to another, and so on.

So already you've got five items you can send out. But maybe you don't want to send them out, because your release has already broken (been printed) in the columnist's paper and you know he wouldn't want to repeat the same thing. But you know he does use items of this sort, so you rummage around, and come up with something like these:

Orvaline Wynette will contribute her prize-winning coconut drop cookies to the May 4th PTA Bake Sale at Jacksonville Elementary School.

*

Cakes, pies, and cookies representing the recipes of twelve different nations will be on sale at the Jacksonville Elementary School PTA Bake Sale on May 4th.

42 pies, 65 cakes, and more than five gross of cookies will be for sale at the PTA Bake Sale, May 4th at Jacksonville Elementary School.

*

30 members of the PTA are donating their services to the Bake Sale this Monday (May 4th) at Jacksonville Elementary School.

*

Of the 30 members of the PTA donating their services to the Bake Sale this Monday (May 4th) at Jacksonville Elementary School, four will be tending the doors, two will be stationed in the hallways to seek out new members for the PTA, and also to direct the way to the gymnasium, where the event is being held, 18 will be behind the counters, four will be behind the "cash register," and two will "float" throughout the event, contributing their services where needed.

*

May Lou McCheechie is the biggest single contributor to the annual PTA Bake Sale at Jacksonville Elementary School May 4th. She'll be furnishing twelve pies, two cakes, and 144 cookies.

Those are the straight news items. But even a bake sale can have its humorous aspects, so here are an anecdote and a joke, to show you how to do it next time you're chosen to publicize an event:

Wiluda Meyer, who's in charge of that May 4th PTA Bake Sale at Jacksonville Elementary School, had a harrowing experience the other night. She had a nightmare that someone was trying to break through her bedroom window. She was so frightened that she woke up—and found someone *was* trying to get through her window. It was husband Fred, who'd lost his keys and, when he found the front and back doors locked, climbed up that stately maple tree on the left side of 154 Martense Street.

*

Jane Smith, who's one of those in charge of the May 4th PTA Bake Sale at Jacksonville Elementary School, passes this one on: "What did you get when the mafia boss swam near a shark? 'The Godfather—Part One and Part Two.' "

Let me pause here to mention that the form used to send out a column item is almost exactly like that used in press releases, except that you don't use a headline, and instead of "FOR IMMEDIATE RELEASE, PLEASE," you write "EXCLUSIVE TO ARTHUR BRETSCHNEIMER" (or whatever the columnist's name is).

Back to Art John, the author of "War and Puce." First we'll try a few news items. And, of course, in Mr. John's case any columnist might be interested, since a book—theoretically at least—is available to the whole country. The first item, though, would be aimed at a local New York City columnist:

Brooklyn adman Art John just had his first novel, "War and Puce," accepted. The book, about an interior decorator's adventures in the South Pacific in 1944, will be published September 10th by Bradbury and Son.

*

"War and Puce," a novel to be published September 10th (by Bradbury and Son), took adman Art John ten years to write. The father of twelve children, he had to tend to his family's needs first.

That new novel "War and Puce" was based to a large extent on author Art John's World War II experiences in Fort Dix, New Jersey.

And so on. Now we'll try some anecdotes and a joke or two. Let me state here that the anecdotes and jokes don't have to be original with the client or the press agent (though that's the way I've always worked, simply because I find it more enjoyable). They can simply be anecdotes or jokes that you've heard or read, and feel you can pass on. The following would be examples of non-original material:

Art John, author of the new novel "War and Puce," says about the funniest story he ever heard concerned two drunks who were staggering about town with no idea of what time it was. One looked up at the sky and said, "It'sh nighttime. There'sh the moon." The other lush glanced straight up and gurgled, "You're crazy. It'sh daytime. That'sh the sun." Just then another imbiber came lurching by, and they put it up to him: "Ish that the moon or the sun?" The swaying third party stared upward for a minute or two, and then began moving off, shrugging, "I don't know. I don't come from around here."

*

Art John, author of "War and Puce," says: "Today's baseball stars are less concerned about their batting averages than about the Dow-Jones averages."

Back to our friend Mumbles Branigan, the disk jockey. As a local celebrity, news from him can be particularly welcome, since the columnist knows that his readers may very well be interested in events in Mr. Branigan's life. Straight news items are fine, and so are jokes and anecdotes, but zany-though-real items about Mr. Branigan would be the most welcome and have the most impact.

I think you've got the idea by now on the first three categories, so here are a few more colorful news items that might be sent out about Mumbles:

Mumbles Branigan, KAWA's madcap disk jockey, claims to be the only DJ in town with five different-colored toupees, black, red, brown, blond, and gray. Matches his toupee to the girl he's going out with.

*

KAWA's Mumbles Branigan decided to lift our local fire-fighters' morale. So he sent them a sign that, instead of reading austerely, "Fire House," bears the warmer-sounding "Fire Home."

*

Mumbles Branigan claims to have the only existing copy of "Goonmlow" by the Five Quadruplets on the Drecca label. "It's rare, but not expensive," the KAWA jock explains. "The record's so bad, nobody else wants it."

*

Mumbles Branigan is running a "sound-alike" contest on his morning KAWA show. The winner will be interviewed on his show, but "Anybody who sounds like Robert Goulet has to leave town."

*

Mumbles Branigan says he got rid of his Venus flytrap at KAWA. Decided he missed the flies more than he liked the plant.

*

Mumbles Branigan, KAWA's house crazy, had three beauties

with him when he dined last night at the Villa Froid. "One on each arm," as Branigan explained it.

*

Mumbles Branigan, KAWA's morning DJ, is running a "Why I Love to Be a Housewife" contest. Contestants have to write a letter in thirty words or less, and are guaranteed anonymity in case of reprisals from ultra-militant Women's Libbers. Neatness will count, but peanut butter and jelly stains on the letter or envelope will not be held against you.

For the press agent trying to get publicity for a local theater company, that bio form we showed you in Chapter 8 can be helpful. Even more helpful, if you've got the time, is talking to all the members of the cast, and all the people behind the scenes, right down to the ticket-takers and sweeper-uppers. I remember back in the 1960s when I handled publicity for *Gogo Loves You,* an Off-Broadway musical by Anita Loos, the largely unknown cast got plenty of newspaper space, simply because we were able to send out one column item after another on them.

The items tended to run to anecdotes about an actor's hairpiece or slightly offbeat facts about the people involved with the show. Exotic hobbies, oddball statistics (perhaps in a cast of fourteen, twelve of the actors are left-handed), personal eccentricities (I've broken more than one item on the fact that Woody Allen is very nervous about having his shoes off) are the stuff of column items, just as much as straight news, jokes, and anecdotes.

Thus, virtually anything—any event, any person, any business —can be publicized via the column item. A local grocery man can become a "character," and thus attract more business, if his gags pop up from time to time in local columns. A celebrity auction has a column item at hand every time it receives one more article from a celebrity. Don Ameche's telephone, a signed autographed picture from Lassie, a still-unopened bottle of water that belonged to W. C. Fields—all can be used as column items. For a restaurant, a new dish on its menu, a new cook, a new headwaiter, a change in decor can become items as well as news releases.

Often things with column-item potential stare you right in the face and you never realize it. You've got to attune your mind to going after column items. Just sitting down and thinking hard for fifteen minutes or so will frequently give you a raft of items, items that had been in your mind all the time, that had been a part of your knowledge, but simply hadn't been translated from known fact into potential news.

One last word on the column item. Most of them don't work. Columnists receive much news, and of course generate their own, so they're not usually hurting for anything. But what one columnist doesn't see fit to print, another may.

So if after three or four weeks your item hasn't broken, you have a choice. You can send it to the same columnist again, because it's possible that at the time you wrote him he didn't need material and either threw your item away unread or merely glanced at it before tossing it. It's also possible that what didn't catch his fancy the first time, might now. I have on occasion sent a columnist a joke by a client a third or fourth time, because I felt it was a good joke and couldn't figure out why he didn't use it. He ignored it, didn't need it, or didn't find it funny those first two or three times, but on the last try—voilà! My client's joke (and name!) in the papers!

So that's your first choice. The second, and one that's usually taken, is to send the item to another columnist. One man's poison can be another's poisson, and frequently columnists are delighted to receive (and use) items that another (or many others) had disdainfully discarded. If you do take this latter course, send out the item or items the way you did the first time, with the same heading, only this time reading "EXCLUSIVE TO" whoever the new columnist is. You're not fudging here. It *is* exclusive, because the first fellow obviously isn't going to use it, and since no one else has it . . .

So don't give up on an item. Persistence, persistence, persistence—that's what publicity is all about. Or have I already told you that?

SUMMARY

1. Gear your items to the kind of things that turn up in the column you're sending them to.

2. Use the usual block in the upper left corner—name, address, telephone number.

3. Write "EXCLUSIVE TO RED EMBRAY," or whoever the columnist might be, in the place where you'd normally type "FOR IMMEDIATE RELEASE, PLEASE."

4. Be imaginative, resourceful, persistent in gathering your column items.

5. If items don't break with one columnist, try another. And if no one uses them, come up with more.

6. Send out many, many items to increase your chances, since most of them won't break.

11

Photos

The most important thing to remember about taking photos is that your photographer is a dunce. The second most important thing to remember is not to tell him so.

In all the years I've been in publicity I've been constantly amazed at how little photographers who take publicity pictures know about them. There must be some who really know their stuff, but I can only recall meeting one.

So it's your job to make sure that the photographer does his job. Never, *never,* NEVER assume he knows what he's doing.

Well, hardly ever. The picture that's used most often in publicity is the stock photograph known as a "head shot." This is simply a portrait of an entertainer or whoever that shows him/her from the shoulders or neck up. What I've said above doesn't really apply to this category. Most of the people who take head shots have been in the business awhile and have learned what works and what doesn't. The most important thing to remember, though, if you're working with a photographer who hasn't done much of this before, is that you're safest if you use a white background. The subject stands out in front of a white background, whereas a dark background can tend to swallow parts of him up. The reproduction in a newspaper is frequently second-rate. Thus, a picture that may reproduce badly often isn't used at all. The picture of singer Lora Lee Cliff (page 142) is a perfect shot to send out to newspapers. Crisp, clear, with a white background, it'll reproduce anywhere.

The picture of singer Ann Johnson (page 143), though artistically far superior, is a little more dubious. It's worked for me in the past when she's appeared at Dangerfield's nightclub, but the darker background and the artistic white highlight on her hair worried me before I sent it out. If I had my choice, I'd take Lora Lee's picture any time for newsprint. There's no question that Ann's shot would do best with magazine editors, but if most of the time it's newsprint you're after, go for the simpler shot.

Sometimes a full-length picture is needed, and on page 144, with singer Eloise Laws, we see why a white background is much more effective. In the picture on page 145, so much of Eloise's head (dark hair, shadows on the face) would disappear into the background in most newspapers, that she would be almost lost, so most newspaper Picture Editors wouldn't consider using this shot. On the picture with the white background, however, she stands out perfectly, and I had good luck with this one when I was handling Eloise's publicity.

Group pictures present another kind of problem, and this is one of the problems photographers, no matter how many pictures they've taken for newspapers, seem to be completely unaware of. The problem is . . . empty space. Most of the time, when people stand together, they give each other plenty of breathing space. On a social level this may be the most comfortable position, but in a news picture it can wreak havoc. A Photo Editor abhors large, unmeaningful areas in his pictures. He's usually tight for space, and a picture that's not compactly arranged takes more space than he may feel it's entitled to. So he doesn't use it.

When you take a picture of a group of people (whether the PTA committee or a scene from your theater group's latest production), get the people close together. I mean close. Ascloseasthis, as Walter Winchell used to say. Cheek by jowl is what I usually tell the people as I try to arrange them, and I mean actually that close when it comes to two people together. Arrangement is a little tougher when more than two people are involved, but get them

LORA LEE CLIFF

ANN JOHNSON

ELOISE LAWS

Barry Kramer

ELOISE LAWS

close, even physically moving them together if you have to. Shoulders should be touching, at the very least. Don't depend on the photographer to do it. He won't.

Again, when you're taking a group photo for newspaper reproduction, get them against a light-colored (preferably white) background. A blank wall is usually best, and certainly the easiest to find.

With a theatrical shot, of course, there often is no light background, or the director wants the shot taken where it occurs in the show. In that case, just be sure, if you're dealing with an amateur photographer, that he has all the light possible going for him. With a professional, check with him to find out how much equipment he'll be bringing (in some cases, this also serves as a reminder to him that he'll need it) and what kind of electric outlet it needs (110 or 220), and then check beforehand for outlets so he'll be able to set up quickly.

I've never been involved in a cheesecake-shooting session, worse luck, but I think I've slavered over enough girlie pictures to give you a few tips. Cheesecake will possibly soon be a fading phenomenon, what with the advent of Women's Liberation. However, so far I see no signs of it, and there is *nothing* that brings quicker results in publicity than a great cheesecake shot. It can turn up anywhere in a newspaper—on the amusement page, on the photo page, in the centerfold, in a column, on a news page, even on the front page. And it needs less news justification than anything else in the newspaper. People like to look at attractive women. It's as simple as that.

The usual cheesecake shot, as we all know, tries to get away with as little clothing as the law allows, and highlights bust, legs, face, hips or derriere, and belly, in about that order. The long-legged look is always in, so, as you'll notice in virtually any cheesecake picture you ogle, the woman stands on tiptoe. Somehow it never seems that way and they simply appear to have strikingly long legs. I'm told it helps to have the woman hold her arms tightly against the sides of her breasts, thus accenting the shadow of her cleavage. Certainly this is an area you should point out to your photographer if it doesn't occur to him (and the odds are fifty-fifty it won't, unless he specializes in this kind of shot). Make sure your subject's hair is in place, that she's holding in her stomach if she needs to, have her think lovely thoughts . . . and snap!

A pretty girl is always helpful in any publicity-picture situation. If you're going to have that groundhog turn up on February 2nd in front of your shop, why not hire (or borrow) a pretty girl, in attire as revealing as possible, to let the groundhog out of his burrow? Similarly, if there's to be a ribbon-cutting ceremony, why not have a pretty girl hold the ribbon while the dignitary does the snipping?

It's also wise to remember that photography, like publicity, is pretty much a let's-try-everything-we-can-so-that-something-may-turn-out kind of business. Good photographers take many, many pictures of their subjects. Probably yours will, too, but in case you have a feeling he hasn't taken enough, don't be shy about suggesting an additional snap or two. After all, if you hadn't hired him, he wouldn't have this job.

When the photographer takes his picture, stand as close to him as you can without being in his way, so that you can see just what it is he's taking. That way, if someone has a hair out of place, you'll see it. From another angle you might miss it.

What about taking the pictures yourself? It's always seemed the best of all possible worlds to me, but I've never done it, because photography's not my bag. I don't know any top press agents who do it, possibly because it's not their bag either, but probably because they're just too busy. But if you've got the time, the inclination, and the feeling you can handle it yourself, by all means go to it. Might be a good idea to do a little experimenting beforehand, though, just to save yourself the possible embarrassment of lousing up a whole photo session, taking up everybody's time for nothing, and getting nowhere in the newspapers.

And now a most important point: *Never* send out a picture without a caption attached. Here are a couple of sample captions:

Singer Hardy Perennial will open in the Bach Room of the Hotel Stanhope on Sunday, July 11th, for a two-week engagement. Holding over will be comedian Bertrand ("Bertie") Russell ("Russie") and the Seven Hands Trio.

*

L to R: Myra Nemmo, Betty Burgos, and Mara Everett plan the "Big MN Charity Ball," which will take place on Wednesday, January 13th, in the semi-grand ballroom of the Hotel Hostel.

When you type up a caption, leave plenty of white space at the top, and then, across the page, stretch out your letterhead, thusly:

FROM: SIMONE KIRBY 123 Moldolph Street (212) 555-1212

Then, instead of "FOR IMMEDIATE RELEASE, PLEASE," I always write "SPECIAL." I don't know why, and I don't think the person who told me to do it ever knew why, so I'm not going to push you on this.

Below "SPECIAL" (or blank space, or whatever you prefer to write), type your caption. Then, if you have it, take some rubber cement and spread it over the blank top of your page. Place it under the picture so that only the heading and caption show. If the paper is wider than the picture, grab a pair of scissors and trim the paper. Otherwise, the caption may rip off when it's being taken out of the envelope, and the editor may assume the picture was sent without one. Also trim off any excess paper at the end of the caption. And if you don't have rubber cement, Scotch Tape will do. It's just that editors like to remove the caption before a picture is made up (sent out to be engraved), and a rubber-cemented caption is easier to pull off and less likely to rip the picture in the process.

Once the caption is attached and trimmed, fold it over the picture so it will fit in the envelope, and put a piece of cardboard backing in the envelope so that the picture won't be bent (and thus useless, since they crack) in the mail.

A final word. Pictures that go out to newspapers are almost invariably 8 × 10 glossies—that is, sized eight inches by ten inches, and printed with a glossy, rather than a matte, finish.

HOW TO ATTACH A PICTURE CAPTION

There was a time when the less-monied newspapers would only print a picture if they were furnished with a mat—a cardboard reproduction of the photograph which could be printed from directly. However, with the advent of photo-offset, these papers seem to be disappearing; may, indeed, have disappeared already. In any case, after sending out your pictures, when you follow up you'll know soon enough if the papers use mats. They'll tell you, and if you pursue it just a bit further, they'll also tell you where you can have them made up.

Do check to find out if your pictures have been received. If they haven't been, you'll never know unless you call. If they have been, it gives you a chance to talk to the editor and perhaps convince him to use your picture rather than someone else's. A simple, buoyant "Hope you can use it" does the trick more often than you'd think it would.

SUMMARY

1. It's your job as a press agent to make sure publicity pictures are taken correctly. Make sure people in a group picture are close together so there is no space between them. Try to get your pictures taken in front of a light-colored (preferably white) background.

2. Attractive women are space-grabbers. Whenever you can use one, do so.

3. Try to visualize the picture the photographer is taking by standing near him and even, if necessary, framing the picture with your hands.

4. Caption all your pictures. In group pictures, a simple "L to R" can be used, instead of "left to right."

5. Send out your pictures to the proper editor, and then *follow up*. That little phone conversation can often make or break your picture release. If you think it's important enough to follow up on it, it makes it just that much more important to the editor.

12

Rejection

As I've intimated along the way, sending something to a newspaper does not automatically signal its eventual triumphant entry into print. Talent-coordinators can have a way of uncoordinating you. Sometimes the most exciting thing about a publicity stunt is that no one at all showed up for it.

Publicity is full of rejection. Chock full of it. Crammed with it. For everything you try, it's possible that one, two, three, eight, sixteen things will fail.

A professional press agent may send out twenty column items a week on a client. He's thrilled if three of them are printed.

A news release about an upcoming event may die a death that would interest a Goya. Five talent-bookers in a row may sigh in your face.

It's all part of the business, and it's something you've got to expect. Or, better yet, not expect but resign yourself to when it happens.

Even better still, don't resign yourself to it, but instead say to yourself, "Okay, what can I do to make it work? And if it won't work where I've approached, where can I turn that it will work?"

It's possible that when the Beatles first came to the United States, their press agent wasn't turned down by anyone. It's possible that when Elizabeth Taylor and Richard Burton married (the first time) their press agent experienced no rejections. Possible, but I wouldn't bet on it. And they were, in their way, phenomena. Most of the time you're not dealing with phenomena. Far from it.

Furthermore, you're dealing with a wide assortment of people when you seek publicity. People, if you'll forgive my stating the obvious, are very, very different. What appeals to one man may infuriate another, while a third may be absolutely indifferent to it. You can't expect your bake sale to generate sympathy with everyone. Your career and caprices as a disk jockey, while delighting one columnist, may evoke nothing but a toss in the wastebasket from another. As a publicist, you're dealing with human nature, not machines, and human nature is even quirkier than the most complex of computers. You can't win 'em all.

But you can win a lot of 'em and, in the process of doing so, salve all the wounds picked up along the way. Let's see how it can be done, demonstrating with that famous bake sale.

Suppose you've sent off your release and no one has used it. What to do?

Send it out again, and if you didn't follow up the first time, follow up now. You'll probably get some results.

What if you don't? Figure out more items to send to the local columnists. Send out a new release with a different news angle. Send out pictures of the people involved.

Call all the local TV and radio shows and see what help you can get there. Try to get them to list you on news shows that contain news of community events. Find out which of your PTA members might have an interest or a talent that would qualify them for an appearance on any of the local interview shows. Make sure, when you book them, that the people responsible for the show know that you'd like to have your bake sale mentioned.

What if you've tried all this and nothing has happened?

Try to come up with more news about the bake sale, and send off a new release. Come up with more column items. Try the pictures again. If you've got new ones, or can take them, send them out.

If you've been turned down by a TV or radio show with one

of your PTA members, suggest another who might be more right for the show.

You mean you haven't been in touch with the women's or family or beauty or fashion page of your newspaper? Surely there are women in your organization who would qualify for an interview. Just make sure that when they're interviewed, the reporter knows you'd like that damned bake sale mentioned.

Still having trouble? What about a bake-sale contest, with the most beautiful, the biggest, the smallest, the most complicatedly made cake, pie, or cookies getting a prize? Send out a release about that.

Still having trouble? Why not send out a piece of cake along with your release, column items, picture, bio, or what have you? Probably by this time, with all you've already tried, you won't need this ploy, but if not—well, maybe no one has ever been seduced by a book, but a piece of chocolate cake . . .

Some years ago a singing duo was opening in New York at a nightclub some of the papers, as policy, didn't ever cover. The singing act had a friend, a very lovely, very charming blonde who agreed to act as their press agent. She personally went to all of the papers, bringing along pictures, releases, and bios of her clients. The space she got! It was unbelievable! If you've got the time, it can't hurt to take your material to the editors in person. And if you're not beautiful and meltingly appealing, but you know someone who is, and who'd be willing to do a little leg work . . .

The point is, the best way of dealing with rejection is following it up with success. In publicity, if you try enough things, you're almost certain to be successful with some of them. All you've got to do is persevere, think creatively, try absolutely everything you can.

My wife has often said that clients get what they deserve. I think by and large that's true, and the thought has certainly saved me some grief when a campaign has turned out to be less than a smashing success. Almost invariably it's been a campaign for a client who didn't deserve that kind of success. So if your bake-sale publicity doesn't do all you (or your officers) had hoped it would do, console yourself with this: It probably wasn't much of a bake sale, anyway.

SUMMARY

Don't give up. Try it all again, and try every new avenue you can conceive of. And then try all that again.

13

Publicity Stunts

There was a time when the publicity stunt was the king of the hill. The man who sold refrigerators to Eskimos, the *Tarzan* promoter who brought a lion into his hotel room—this was what people thought about when they thought about publicity.

But that was back in the earlier days of the century. Came the 1950s and the McCarthy era and "the silent generation," and things began to change. Newspaper editors no longer seemed, as a rule, to be captivated by the outrageous stunt, and were not excited even about the more usual sort of stunt.

Today they're a little more receptive, but not much more. On the other hand, TV news editors are suckers for stunts, judging by the idiocy that often claims their channels. TV news shows need, or at any rate feel the need for, fillers, and a good visual stunt fills the bill of light news that's fun to watch.

There are some stunts that are classic and used year after year. The groundhog gambit I mentioned earlier is one of them. Having a good-looking woman shown turning back a clock or turning it ahead, depending on whether it's Standard or Daylight Saving Time that's coming up, often grabs space. The woman can be the star of a movie, an employee of a company, a member of an organization, a model representing a restaurant, a nightclub, or what-have-you. Almost invariably the client she represents will be mentioned in the caption.

Sometimes you can tie in with another event. When I handled the Greenwich Village club called the Bitter End, we were approached to have a poetry-reading contest there (Greenwich Village in those days being the home of poets), with one of the poets to be a young up-and-coming fighter named Cassius Clay, who was noted for reading poems before his bout in which he'd name the round his opponent would fall. There was a newspaper strike at the time, but we still were able to get quite a turnout, all of which publicized both the Bitter End and Clay's next big fight at Madison Square Garden.

Another time we were handling publicity for the Noël Coward musical *Sail Away,* and a boat show was about to begin at the New York Coliseum. One boat to be displayed there was so big that it couldn't come through the tunnels to Manhattan and had to be specially taken across one of the bridges. So we arranged for several of the pretty dancers of the show to be on board the boat while it was being towed across the bridge and through the streets of New York. At least one local paper gave us extensive coverage, publicizing both the boat show and *Sail Away.*

A pie-eating contest can be a stunt, or a dance marathon, flagpole-sitting, a beauty contest—virtually anything under the sun, as long as it seems interesting. If you've designed a motor that runs twice as far on the same amount of gasoline, a contest between your car and another would be a stunt. The cast of a show dressing in costume and parading through the streets to publicize the opening of their show can be a stunt. A disk jockey staying awake longer than anyone else in history is a stunt. In fact, a good place to look for stunt ideas is the *Guinness Book of Records.* It'll either give you a record to shoot for or stimulate some ideas of your own.

There is one problem about stunts, and that's why I've stayed away from them for the most part during my years in publicity. When they don't work, when no one turns up, you're left with an awful lot of time totally and completely wasted, as well as with a good bit of egg on your face. If you've got nothing else to do anyway, fine, give it a go. But if there are all sorts of other things you can be doing to publicize whatever you're representing, my suggestion would be to get those things done first. Most stunts take up an inordinate amount of time. There's the brainstorming, the gathering together of all the elements needed in the stunt, the releases, the calls, the time away from the office while the stunt's going on. It can all add up to many, many hours.

However, as I say, don't disregard the stunt entirely. It can have enormous potency, and that's why so many people turn to it, despite the ever present danger of total and abysmal failure.

Since these days the television cameras are the thing you think about first when planning a stunt, try to fit the stunt into the time that's best for them. Call your local station or stations, find out when they prefer to send a crew out. Afternoons are usually best, Sundays usually worst because there is often no news show on Sunday night and crews are smaller that day. But check your own stations first. Their hours may be somewhat different.

When you have a stunt arranged, write a press release and have copies made. Then start calling the news desks of newspapers, television, radio, and, if it'd be of interest to them, wire services and syndicates, magazines and trade journals.

After you've contacted them, send out your release (which should name time, place, etc.) to those who are interested. Then follow up to make sure the release has arrived, and finally, unless you're warned not to, or you sense it would be one call too many, make a confirming call on the day of the event. And then—good luck! You do have one ace in the hole in the case of a failed publicity stunt. If the client is willing to pay for a photographer, you can take your own pictures and then service them (properly captioned) to the news desks. More than one stunt has been saved this way.

It's also helpful to be aware of days that may be so full of news that no one would be interested in your story. Certainly keep away from stunts on Election Day, or when the President is coming to town. All the available cameras will be used for these events plus the usual essential news.

Once again, let me state that if you can get a beautiful woman (the more skin showing, the better) into your stunt, the better chance you'll have, both in enticing people to cover it, and in having your stunt, once covered, given the editor's approval for use in his newspaper, on his show, or whatever.

Keeping upcoming events in mind can be helpful. The first day of winter, the birthday of a President, the anniversary of a local battle can help set up a stunt. A stunt, if you're going to give it the best shot it can have, should be rooted in something. A disk jockey going for a non-sleep record would be meaningless if he weren't also trying to play records at the same time. A pretty girl turning back a clock would be ludicrously pointless if we weren't all going to be turning back our clocks. So be brilliant, be creative, be outrageous, but at the same time try to have your stunt rooted in some kind of reality. That'll be giving it your best shot.

SUMMARY

1. Only do a stunt if you've got the time or you're sure it's got an excellent chance of doing well, or if it's simply the best way you can see of getting publicity.

2. Thinking in visual terms is helpful, particularly to entice TV cameras, but also for the picture desks of newspapers and magazines. Have your stunt, no matter how zany, grounded in reality.

14

The Press Conference

The press conference can be a wonderful publicity tool. In one fell swoop you get your message across. No call after call, no interview after interview, no news release after news release. It's all taken care of at once. Bam. What could be simpler?

Unfortunately, there is a hitch. To be worthy of a press conference, the subject of the conference has to be of wide interest and an interest strong enough to convince the press to arrange their schedules around it.

Most of you who are reading this book will have no need ever to arrange a press conference. Even as a professional for many years, I have only been involved with a handful. However, for those who may find it helpful, here's what a press conference is all about, and here's how it's handled.

First, as I've indicated, be sure that you've got an event or an announcement that will interest a sizable portion of the press. Next, pick a date that will give you the best chance of drawing the press. Saturday and Sunday are not good because many press people don't work on those days, and not many of them would like to come by on their day off. Monday is generally bad because it's usually a very busy day for the press, as they dig out from the news, mail, etc., that's accumulated over the weekend. Then you've got to keep an eye out for other news events that may break on the day you're planning your conference. If someone in town is going to be making a major speech, or an exciting new product is to be unveiled, or a movie star will be holding a press conference, stay away from that day.

Next (and this is crucial, obviously, but people sometimes forget to do it), check with your client, once you've found a suitable date, and make sure it's okay with him.

Then it's time to decide on where you're going to hold the conference. If you don't have a place immediately handy, you'll have to start checking hotels, catering halls, restaurants, to see what they've got available, and what it's going to cost you. In this electronic age, be certain to find out in advance if the room you'll be holding the conference in has enough electrical outlets. If you think you'll need sound equipment for your speaker or speakers, check its availability. Don't forget tables for the speakers, and chairs for everyone. I might add that free liquor and food can sometimes attract press, so if you can provide them, do so, and make sure you let the press know it in advance.

Once you've got the hall, the date, and the time of day, it's time to write your release, which is set up the same way you write a release for any event, addressed to the news desks (even though you will almost undoubtedly be sending it to others as well), and using the Who, What, Where, When, and Why formula.

A sample press-conference release could read like this:

FROM: ROGER BYRD
        123 Wuxtry Street
        Hot Flash, Maryland 21032
        (205) 555-1212

ATTENTION: NEWS DESKS

NOTED PHILOSOPHER TO DISCLOSE MEANING OF LIFE

Rhodes Reagan, the noted philosopher, will disclose the meaning of life in a press conference to be held this Monday

(December 10th) at 10 A.M. in the Grand Ballroom of the Hotel Overton.

Reagan, perhaps the most noted philosopher of our time, has decided to disclose the meaning of life at this press conference, in advance of the publication of his book, "Life: Its Meaning."

There will be a buffet and bar for attending press.

EVENT: Rhodes Reagan to disclose meaning of life.

WHERE: Grand Ballroom of the Hotel Overton, 453 Lenox Road

WHEN: Monday (December 10th)

TIME: 10 A.M.

CONTACT: Roger Byrd, (205) 555-1212

Once the release is written and reproduced, get on the phone. Call everyone who could possibly be interested. This would usually include the newspaper city desks, the radio and television news shows, any local columnist whose beat it would possibly fall into, trade journals, and if it's big enough news to attract national coverage, then you'd also go after the wire services, the syndicates, and the magazines.

If the client is going to give a speech and that's the reason for the conference, then have copies of the speech made up so that they can be given to all the press at the conference. If it's not to be a speech, then write a story giving the basic facts to be disclosed at the conference and hand it to the press as they arrive or as they leave, so they can refer to it while doing their stories. This can be double-spaced or single-spaced, whichever makes it fit more attractively onto the page (preferably a single page and hopefully no more than two—anything more than this becomes

cumbersome for anyone planning to write a standard news story).
Don't forget to include your name, address, and phone number.

Two or three days after you've sent out your release, check
the press to make sure they've received it, and to find out if they
plan to attend.

Depending on what time you've set the conference for, make
one last call to the press, either the day before or the morning of
the event, to confirm that the event is taking place and that they
will be coming.

Get to the conference hall or room ahead of time, to make sure
that everything that's supposed to be there is there and in working
order.

When the time comes for the press to arrive, station yourself
or your assistants at the door, greet them, introduce yourself, and
find out who they are and where they're from. This is partly just
plain politeness, and partly because it helps to get to know
the press personally. It may help you with this story, and it
can be valuable in the future. Nobody from the press is ever going to do you a favor just because they know and like you, but
they may turn a more sympathetic ear at least. Don't forget to
hand them the background material, and also see if you can get
an idea as to when they plan to run the story, so that you can pull
it out when it runs.

It's your job to let the speaker know when to begin, and usually
it's the press agent who introduces the speaker.

Once the conference is over, make sure everyone has the press
material he needs, then make sure that you're the last one out
and that any equipment you're responsible for is taken care of.

That's all there is left for you to do at the press conference.
But you still have a big responsibility, and that's to keep track of
everything that runs. Keep flicking the dials when the news
shows are on (or have friends or associates monitor one show while
you're watching another), and follow up on what's due to be seen
in print. If for some reason the story doesn't run, call up and see
if it will be run at another time, or, if not, if there's some way you
can resurrect the story.

SUMMARY

1. Make sure you've got a story that will attract the press to a conference.

2. Pick a date that is good for the press and doesn't conflict, if possible, with other events that will rate press coverage.

3. Once you've picked the date, make sure your client knows it, and that it's okay with him.

4. Find a place to hold the conference. Make certain there are chairs for the press, a podium for your speaker, and whatever electric devices are needed.

5. Write a release.

6. Call everyone who might be interested.

7. Send out the release.

8. Follow up on it.

9. Make up copies of your client's speech or a fact sheet to give to the press.

10. Check the press again just before the conference—either the day before or that morning.

11. Get to the place ahead of time and make sure all the equipment you need is there.

12. Greet the press, give them their information either at the beginning or the end, and start the conference when it's time.

13. Be the last to leave, and make sure all equipment has been returned to wherever it's supposed to go.

14. Follow up on the news stories.

15

When Not to Look for Publicity

There is only one time when you should at all costs avoid looking for publicity. That is when you have nothing to publicize.

This seems like a simple truth, but over the years I've had to turn down scores of people who attempted to fly in the face of this essential fact.

Someone, for instance, may decide he wants to be a singer. He calls up a press agent and says, "I'm a singer. I want to be a big star. Publicize me."

How?

To publicize someone or something, you must have a hook, something that makes that someone or something news. If a singer has a nightclub booking, a record, a TV appearance coming up, then that singer can be publicized. But if that singer simply *is,* and has nothing coming up in his career, and nothing currently happening, then he simply can't be publicized.

Well, yes, he *can,* a little bit. He can be used as the person who lets the groundhog out of the cage, can turn ahead the clock come Daylight Saving Time—in short, figure in a stunt here and there. And if he has enormous amounts of money, he can plaster the town with his likeness, on billboards, fences, on TV commercials for himself. Out of this he might get something, but the odds are tremendously against it.

Writing a book and then publicizing it in the hope it will attract a publisher is going about the whole thing the wrong way. Write the book, land a publisher, and then, if you feel your publisher's publicity department isn't going to push your book hard (and with all the books they've got to publicize, there's a good chance they won't), it's time to hire a press agent. Or publicize it yourself.

Unless you can come up with something brilliantly outrageous, there's no reason for you to seek publicity as a disk jockey unless you're already working as a disk jockey. That's the time to capitalize on what you have—to let even more people know about you so that your show will attract a wider following, more commercials, and more money and perhaps a better time slot or station for you.

The news media are interested in news. It's much, much easier to publicize the news value in something that is either happening or about to happen.

So if you don't have anything to publicize, don't embarrass yourself. It's no fun being turned down by the press, and it's even worse if you wind up feeling like an idiot as well. A man who calls up a talk show and says "I want to come on because I know someday I'm going to be a big star" is going to evoke nothing much more than Stella-call-the-booby-hatch-quick from the man at the other end of the phone.

So before you decide it's time to start publicizing something, take stock of what it is you want to publicize. Does it have news value? That's the main question. It doesn't have to have earth-shattering news value. That ever-cited PTA bake sale is not exactly a stop-the-presses item, but it *is* news, and is therefore legitimately publicizable.

The same for a one-night booking as a singer in a small local nightclub. Again not quite like winning a Grammy, but it's news, and releases can be sent, pictures can be sent, column items can be sent, press, TV, and radio interviews can possibly be arranged, critics can be invited. That's not to say that all of these things will get results, of course, but they can legitimately be tried, and the odds are, if you try hard enough, some of them will.

Another time not to look for publicity is when you're looking in the incontestably wrong place. To be booked into a nightclub and ask for a story on the business page would of course be imbecilic, unless there were some business angle in your booking (for instance, if you were a prominent local businessman, or had an enormous following of businessmen, or had taken the $1,000,000 profit you made in the stock market and invested it in a nightclub act). It is good to be enterprising and imaginative when seeking publicity outlets, but it's a waste of time for you and everybody concerned when you look for it in blatantly wrong places.

There is one exception to all of this, obviously, and that is the person or product who is newsy simply by *being*. The fact that Elizabeth Taylor went shopping in such-and-such a store or is thinking about becoming an artist is news, simply because Elizabeth Taylor has reached the position where she is *always* news.

As I've mentioned previously, there is another area in which one should tread lightly. If you're going to publicize an event, it's always a good idea, if there's any way you can arrange your date, to check ahead and see if any similar event is scheduled for that date. If so, increase your chances for coverage by changing your date. Movie producers do it, Broadway producers do it, professional press agents do it. You should, too.

SUMMARY

1. Make sure you've got something to publicize before you try publicizing it.

2. Try to plan your publicity so that it doesn't conflict with an event of a like nature—that is, opening a play on the same night that another play is to open.

16

Other Avenues of Promotion

Recently, in New York, a relatively unknown young singer named Peter Lemongello became something of a star performer by a simple expedient: he spent $180,000 on TV commercials to sell his privately produced album. Not only did he make all his money back, and more, through selling his albums—he twice sold out the 2,825-seat Avery Fisher Hall at Lincoln Center and was recognized wherever he went. He was also signed by a record company, and received numerous nightclub offers and television guest spots. He did hire a press agent to help exploit all this, but his press agent would agree, I'm sure, that the sales of the album, the sellout of the hall, and his sudden celebrity came about strictly through that barrage of commercials It was a bright idea and (thanks in large part to all that money behind him) it worked.

There are, thus, many ways in which things can be promoted. Advertising, of course, is a basic approach. Bill-posting is another. All one need do is figure out where the posters should be placed, have them printed, and then post them. In some cases this can be done legally, and usually no one minds when a non-commercial enterprise does some bill-posting of its own. However, since bill-posting is often frowned on legally, a semi-subterranean trade has sprung up, at least in some of the big cities. This trade is known as "sniping," and "snipers" are men who, in the dead of night, roll up to fences, buildings, anywhere they can glue on a poster, and slap them on before anyone's the wiser.

Direct mailing is another means, and door-to-door solicitation another. I don't think these need any explanation. Just keep them in mind for your enterprise in case they apply.

One way of getting personal publicity is through the radio and television public-service commercial. Charities are given a certain amount of free time on radio and television to plead their causes, and often these organizations find their messages are more effective if delivered by someone who is known to the public.

Of course, anyone reading this book who plans to publicize himself is not likely to be famous enough to be accepted for a national public-service spot. But often the local organizations for charities do their own spots, and local celebrities may be right for them—a locally known politician, an author, an entertainer, etc. Just call them and find out. And, by the way, charity doesn't only mean organizations that aid the poor—it encompasses foundations that battle specific illnesses, drug rehabilitation centers, religious organizations, ecological groups, mental-health centers, etc. The best way to check them out is through the yellow pages of your phone book, under the listing "Social Service Organizations."

Another avenue of publicity is through your own writing. Sometimes when you approach an editor with a story and he tells you he'd like to print something about it but can't spare a reporter, you can ask him if he'd mind your trying your hand at writing it. It's not a frequent occurrence, but it can happen that an editor will say yes, and sometimes even run the story with your byline. If you do get such an opportunity, read over the newspaper first to get a sense of its style. If you're writing a feature interview, make sure there are plenty of good quotes, and if it's a straight news story, use quotes wherever you can. Quotes enliven a story and can even save yours, since they are the meat and potatoes of much news copy and an experienced editor can quickly repair the framework that supports them.

Finally, there are promotional gimmicks that can garner a lot of publicity mileage for you or your client.

Often, to publicize a client's nightclub opening, press agents invite other celebrities to the opening, free, in the hope that the event will seem more prestigious and collect more space in the columns.

Your PTA bake sale will have just that much more going for it if it's known that people of prominence will be in attendance—a congressman, a state senator, the mayor, a local singing group, etc. If you're a disk jockey and you know you'll be interviewing Bob Dylan in a week or two, that news is worth sending out. An inventor planning to unveil his newest brainstorm will attract more attention if he can announce that several prominent scientists will be in attendance. Politicians seem to find the well-publicized support of celebrities helpful.

Contests can be a good gimmick if your organization wants publicity but doesn't at the moment have anything to publicize. Contests can be anything: pie-eating, field and track events, home movie-making, barbershop quartets—anything under the sun that might invite competition. A contest is one of the best ways to get TV news coverage, since it's usually visual and makes for good light entertainment.

An annual award can create news interest for your organization (or yourself, if you decide to create your own foundation). It can be hero-of-the-year, mother-of-the-year, citizen-of-the-year —again, the possibilities are almost endless, and are almost certain to attract attention from the media.

Exhibits of all sorts—art exhibits, flower shows, historical exhibitions—can be used to make the public aware of your organization, and perhaps even rake in a few shekels.

Dedications for new buildings, ground-breaking ceremonies, ribbon-cutting all have their publicity value.

In short, publicity can be a never-ending occupation, even publicity for a single client. There is always one more avenue to explore, one more medium to conquer, one more column item to send out. It all depends on you.

Index

Page numbers in italic refer to illustrations.